Greg will show you how to become a best-selling author to the most important reading audience in the world . . . your family. It just doesn't get any better than that!

DR. STEVE FARRAR
AUTHOR, POINT MAN

Our heavenly Father has written us a personal love letter called the Bible. *Letters From Dad* follows a solid, Biblical model as it teaches men how to write words of faith, hope, and love that will be a blessing to their families for generations to come.

DR. GENE GETZ
AUTHOR, THE MEASURE OF A MAN

My dear friend Greg Vaughn has found a shiny, new lure called *Letters From Dad* that hooks the hearts of men, helping them say the things they've always wanted to say but just didn't know how.

DR. H. NORMAN WRIGHT
AUTHOR, SO YOU'RE GETTING MARRIED

The book *The Blessing* taught us what it was. *The Prayer of Jabez* taught us how to pray it. *Letters From Dad* shows us how to speak, write, and give the blessings of God to those you love.

BYRON WILLIAMSON
PRESIDENT, INTEGRITY PUBLISHING

Letters From Dad is Promise Keepers on steroids!

TOM DOOLEY
NATIONAL RADIO HOST

Do you have a letter of blessing from your father? If you're like me you don't, but if you did there would be only one word to describe it . . . priceless. There's a new ministry emerging that is capturing the hearts of fathers throughout the country. It's called *Letters From Dad*. Men, it will change your lives!

DR. KEN CANFIELD
THE NATIONAL CENTER FOR FATHERING

LETTERS FROM DAD

GREG VAUGHN

with FRED HOLMES

INTEGRITY®
PUBLISHERS
Nashville

Published by Integrity Publishers, a division of Integrity Media, Inc., 5250 Virginia Way, Suite 110, Brentwood, TN 37027.

HELPING PEOPLE WORLDWIDE EXPERIENCE the MANIFEST PRESENCE of GOD.

Unless otherwise indicated, Scripture quotations are taken from The Holy Bible, New International Version® (NIV®). Copyright © 1973, 1978, 1984 by International Bible Society. Used by permission of Zondervan. All rights reserved.

Other Scripture quotations are taken from the following: The New King James Version® (NKJV®). Copyright © 1982 by Thomas Nelson, Inc. Used by permission. All rights reserved. The King James Version (KJV). Public domain.

Cover Design: Tobias' Outerwear for Books, Davisburg, MI.
Interior Design: Sharon Collins of Artichoke Design, Nashville, TN.

All photos courtesy of the Pat and Mike Self family, the Strong family, the George Jordan family, and the Greg Vaughn family.

Library of Congress Cataloging-in-Publication Data

Vaughn, Greg (Gregory L.)
 Letters from dad : how to leave a legacy of faith, hope, and love for
your family / by Greg Vaughn with Fred Holmes.
      p. cm.
 Summary: "Letters from Dad helps fathers leave a legacy of faith, hope, and love
to their families in the form of treasured words of love and blessing"—Provided
by publisher.

ISBN 1-59145-342-9 (hardcover)

1. Christian life. 2. Fathers—Religious life. I. Holmes, Fred. II.
Title.

BV4501.3.V38 2005
248.4—dc22
                                              2005008309

Printed in the United States
05 06 07 08 BVG 9 8 7 6 5 4 3 2

Acknowledgments

This book came from the skillful hands of many people . . .

First, I would like to thank my dear friend, Fred Holmes, for taking the words of my mouth and thoughts of my heart and turning them into the book you hold in your hand. It's my prayer that it will be pleasing to my God and a source of blessing to all who read it.

Second, I'd like to express my thanks to my dear wife, Carolyn, for loving me enough to let me chase my dreams, and to my seven precious children for allowing me to so publicly share our lives with others. Always remember, my dear family, you are the treasures of my life.

To Robin Blakeley, I would like to say thanks for cheering me on each and every day of the Letters From Dad adventure, and for seeing that this book became a reality.

To the original fourteen men who so eagerly chose to take the first journey—thanks, guys!

And thanks to all those at Grace Products who encouraged the vision and are a constant source of wisdom and counsel to me. John Strong, your words of wisdom have been a double portion of blessing to me during this time.

I would also like to thank the staff at Integrity Publishing who labored so diligently to bring this book to fruition, with a special thank you to Byron Williamson and Joey Paul for their vision and courage in making this dream a reality. Thanks especially to Angela DePriest and Sharon Collins for their unique creativity in making the book visually exciting.

I would also like to say a special thanks to my mother, Wanda Vaughn, who brought me to the feet of my Savior, and who has prayed for me each and every day of my life; and to my brother, Stephen, for teaching me the meaning of suffering under the mighty hand of God. There is a special crown in heaven for you, Stephen.

And finally, I wish to say a special thanks to my father who left me an old tackle box that held within it a new fishing lure that God is using to hook the hearts of men and help fulfill the promise of Malachi 4:6—to turn the hearts of the fathers to their children and the hearts of children to their fathers. Thanks, Dad. And remember, you owe me a hug.

GREG VAUGHN

Table of Contents

2ND TECHNICAL SCHOOL SQUADRON SPECIAL

LOWRY FIELD, COLORADO

November 10, 194

Darling:

Maybe y...
have gone...
love found...
that you w...
cided to...
didn't wa...
love them...
rite for n...
ecided tha...
my place...
en the starting place for a lot ...
he kids and it has bee...

S/ Sgt Earl E. Vaughn
2nd Tech Sch Sq (4)
Lowry Field, Denver,

DENVER
NOV 11
CO. PM
1942
COLO.

BU...
DEFENSE
BONDS and

Miss Wanda Nelso...
2307 - 7th Street
Lubbock, Texas

❧ Foreword

From this day forward,
I choose to live a life
in honor of my Savior.

I am a father.

And it is my great honor and privilege to serve a large and growing army of men called dads—an army of courageous fathers who have chosen to go on a mission. This isn't a mission for the brave and courageous, but for those who at some time have felt like a complete failure.

As a father my assignment is clear and profound. It affects not only my wife and children but generations not yet born. You see, I've learned that I can make a difference in the lives of my family.

And so can you.

The marching orders of my mission don't come from me, but from God Himself, written in His love letter to us called the Bible. Listen closely to His strong commands:

> *Fathers, open your mouth and utter things of from old . . . things you have heard and know, things your forefathers have told you. Do not hide them from your children. Tell them to the next generation. Tell them of the praiseworthy deeds God has done. Tell of His great power and the great wonders He has done. Teach these things to your children and your grandchildren, so that the next generation will turn and tell their children and their children's children of the love of God. Then they will put their trust in God and never forget His deeds and commands. And why should you do this? So your children will not be like their forefathers who turned from God.* (Psalm 78:1-8, paraphrased)

God has given me a command. As a fellow father, He's given you a command too. The only question is, what will we do with this command? Years ago I vowed to fulfill it. I prayed aloud, "From this day forward, I choose to live a life in honor of my Savior. My passion will be to leave a godly legacy of faith, hope, and love to those precious ones I call my family."

So far it's been an amazing adventure that has changed the heritage of my family. It's my prayer that you will join me in this noble cause. Why? Because it will change your life too. It will change your family. "But I've already made too many mistakes," you say. Remember, if there is breath in your body, there is hope for a new beginning. It starts here. And it starts now.

Take this as an invitation to all fathers—the faint-hearted, the doubtful, the discouraged, even the rejected—to enter this journey with me. We've got our marching orders. The battle is joined. The victory certain.

All that is left to reach the end . . . is to begin.

Hello Darling:
    I didn't die and
t I sure hate te
d all time. I
d a blood clo
asn't bad but if
    taken out it wou
lot of trouble late
    one minute and 59 seconds
        save me a locge and

t Earl E. Vaughn
Feb Sch Sq
ry Fld, Colo.

DENVER
MAY 29
2 7:30 PM
1943
COLO.

BUY
WAR SAVINGS
BONDS AND STAMPS

Miss Wanda Nelson
2307. 7th Street,
Lubbock, Texas

said if I nev
her was going to get Glenda

What was it about this box that could inspire such celebration yet bring such tragedy?

hree thousand years ago, thirty thousand men danced upon a hill.

Thirty thousand men dancing to the sound of lyres, harps, tambourines, castanets, cymbals, and trumpets.

Thirty thousand men dancing with laughter and song.

Their raucous revelry bounced off the mud brick houses of the tiny mountaintop town of Kiriath Jearim, careened through the surrounding forest of fir and cedar, and echoed across the Judean hills all the way to Mount Jearim. They could be heard all the way to the nearby villages of Zorah and Eshtaol, even to Kesla, two miles to the south. Amazingly, their sounds even reached Jerusalem, a full eight miles away.

As if in homage, Kiriath Jearim faced Jerusalem, though both were holy sites. Jerusalem was the holy city upon a hill that God had claimed as His own. Kiriath Jearim also sat upon a hill and was also blessed by God. Twenty years before the town was filled with dancing, God sent a mysterious box to its people, entrusting them with its protection.

And now King David, God's anointed ruler and unifier of all Israel, had come to Kiriath Jearim to reclaim that box and take it home. Wearing a linen ephod, David led the procession that removed the box from the home of Abinadab, whose son, Eleazar, had been charged with its safe keeping. Two of Abinadab's other sons, Uzzah and Ahio, were given the honor of leading the ox-drawn cart that now bore the box through the town streets.

Although the cart was new, it creaked and tottered as it gathered speed descending the steep, rocky hill. It quickly became apparent there was a problem: the cart was going too fast. Only Uzzah and Ahio saw the danger, whipping and yelling at the oxen, while all around them the frenzied celebration continued.

At the bottom of the forested hill lay an ancient graveyard, and by the time the cart passed through the crumbling tombs, it was out of control. The terrified oxen protested with guttural brays as the rampaging cart slammed into the backs of their legs. Uzzah and Ahio whipped them mercilessly, urging them on, but they ignored the whip as their hooves slipped on the rocky terrain.

Then to Uzzah's and Ahio's horror, they saw the threshing-floor of Nacon directly ahead, its polished stone floor smooth as glass. It would be like trying to cross a frozen lake. Reacting instinctively, Ahio grabbed for the oxen's harness while Uzzah ran to steady the cart. They might as well have been trying to stop an avalanche.

The oxen were running full speed when they hit the threshing-floor. As their legs went out from under them, the cart began to tilt, its precious cargo sliding toward the edge. Uzzah put out his hand to stop it. Only then did the surrounding celebrants realize what was happening, and with a shout, they encircled the cart and stopped the disaster before it could go any further.

A sigh of relief went up from David. The unthinkable had almost occurred. Another second and the box would've been destroyed. But relief quickly turned to shock as he saw Uzzah crumpled beside the cart. Thoughts of celebration winnowed away like chaff as David knelt and examined Uzzah's lifeless body. Amazingly, there was not a mark upon him. Not a gash or broken bone. Not one sign of violence.

Uzzah had not been killed by oxen or cart.

He had been killed by God.

Stunned disbelief filled David's eyes—the same eyes that had faced down Goliath and stared into the tortured soul of Saul. The king slowly raised his face to heaven and screamed. "Why?!?"

Why Indeed?

What was it about this box that could inspire such celebration yet bring such tragedy? It was rectangular in shape, measuring about four feet long and two-and-one-quarter feet wide and high. It had been built of acacia wood overlaid with gold, so obviously it had some monetary value. Maybe that's what drew its last owners, the Philistines, to steal it after defeating the Israeli army at the battle of Aphek. The Philistines had kept it for seven months, passing it from town to town.

Why so much moving around? Because everywhere it went, this box was accompanied by plagues. And not just any plagues—bizarre plagues. Plagues of mice and hemorrhoids. That's right, hemorrhoids. In fact, it got so bad that no self-respecting Philistine who wished to sit in comfort would go anywhere near that box. The problem was how to get the Israelis to take it back.

The Philistines came up with an ingenious solution. They had their finest goldsmiths fashion little golden icons resembling mice and hemorrhoids and placed them in a golden box next to the box that had been causing all the problems. They then left both boxes on a cart at the foot of Kiriath Jearim, thinking, *Ha! Now they'll be the ones who'll get hemorrhoids!* But the joke was on the Philistines. The people of Kiriath Jearim didn't get hemorrhoids. As a matter of fact, for the next twenty years they were greatly blessed.

So what was this mysterious box? You've probably already guessed. It was the ark of the covenant. It stood for God's covenant between the Israelites and Himself. It was also called the ark of testimony, reflecting the "testimony" of God's faithfulness to His chosen people.

What made this box so unique was that God Himself dwelt between the two golden cherubim that graced the top. He designated it as the container for His presence among the Jewish people.

But there was also something else. Something inside. Something God greatly prized.

A letter—His first to mankind.

The Ten Commandments

That's right. When the Lord wanted to communicate to us how we could have a relationship with Him, He wrote us a letter. He even handwrote it. He wanted to make it personal. God may have had a sense of humor when it came to the plagues He sent upon the Philistines, but when it came to the Ten Commandments, He was deadly serious. Make no mistake about that. He wanted His people to be guided by every word contained in this letter. Ultimately, it was to be their instruction manual for life.

In fact, with the coming of Jesus Christ and the fulfillment of the Law, He wrote us once again. You've read those letters. They're called the New Testament.

A Forgotten Form

God doesn't take letter writing lightly. Unfortunately, the importance of this fundamental form of communication seems to have been lost on us today—unless you count e-mail, with its electronic shorthand and smiley faces. But snail mail? The old letter in an envelope, with a stamp on the front, entrusted to the United States government? Forget it. Most of us couldn't write a good letter if we were forced to. We promptly forgot what little we learned about good writing sixty seconds after our final English exam.

I know I did. But then again, I didn't have a lot to forget. When it came to writing, I had always aspired to mediocrity and had achieved it with distinction. Just ask any of the English teachers I had throughout my academic years.

"Greg Vaughn, a writer?!?" they'd chuckle. This would be followed by wild, spastic laughter accompanied by red faces and gasps for breath. Can't blame them. I was grammatically challenged. No, I take that back. I was capable of inspired eloquence when the occasion demanded. Unfortunately, the finest prose of my middle school and high school years was forever lost to posterity when some jealous janitor unceremoniously scrubbed it from the bathroom wall.

So you can imagine how shocked my teachers would be today if they knew that their "star" student was now traveling the country encouraging men to write. Heresy! And it gets worse. I'm actually teaching men how to write. Thank goodness my teachers don't know. It could single-handedly raise the heart attack rate across the country.

But I assure you, no one could be more shocked than I. What could possibly encourage such foolishness on my part? Three things: my kids, my dad, and a mystery box of a different kind.

Msgt Earl Vaughn.
Tech Sch Sq
Laury Fld Calif.

POST C

CORRESPONDENCE

Dear Wanda,
    This writing
may not be legable
as I am trying to
write between stops.
Did you get my
card? Write me in
6 days because I
am leaving St. Lou
Monday.
            Love Earl.

If you were to die today,
what would be in the
tackle box of your life?

*B*efore I explain what compelled me to take up something I was notoriously bad at, let me tell you a little about myself. I was born in Lubbock, Texas, in the Texas panhandle. My parents both grew up on rural farms—good ol' West Texas farmland. My dad's father was a sharecropper with twelve children (including my dad) whom he used as slave labor for the farm. Grandfather was a harsh, tough-minded man, and my dad inherited many of those traits.

After my parents married, they moved from the farm to Lubbock to start a family. Not long after came four kids: my older brother, Larry, me, and my two younger brothers, Rick and Steven.

Steven got polio when he was eleven months old, and since this was before the Salk vaccine, he ended up severely affected. Dad didn't handle this well and began to drink heavily and throw himself into his work. Running a community grocery store, he would put in eighteen hours a day, six and sometimes seven days a week.

My mom, on the other hand, was as supportive as a parent could be. She was my hero. Still is. Throughout my childhood, she worked hard at taking care of her home and family, while also working long hours as an RN.

Because of Mom, I accepted Christ into my life when I was six years old. Unfortunately, I ran away from God during my high school and college years. The entire focus of my life had become playing football and chasing girls. But one day during college, my purpose significantly changed when a prominent local businessman came to my fraternity to share the gospel. My first thought was, *This guy's a brave man to come give his testi-*

mony to 120 pagans! I admired him and decided I wanted to be just like him. So when he asked if anyone would like to stick around after the meeting and talk, I did exactly that. From that moment on, my life was turned upside-down again for Christ.

Tackling the Memories

Not long after my father's death I was digging through his things in the garage when I came across an old tackle box that belonged to him. My dad was a rabid fisherman. He loved fishing with a passion. But he rarely took me fishing and never really taught me how to fish.

The last years of my father's life had been difficult, and that tackle box had turned rusty with disuse. It took an oversized screwdriver, some scraped knuckles, and a lot of prying to get it open. Inside I found the usual refuse of a fisherman: worn out lures, dried salmon eggs, rubbery worms fused together, tangled line, and rusty hooks. None of it was of any use to anyone anymore. I carried the box to a nearby garbage can and was preparing to toss it in when suddenly it occurred to me—this was all I had left of my father.

I began to weep. For the life of me, I couldn't have told you why. It was just a rotting mess of useless worms and hooks, but somehow it represented my father—the same father who had never told me he loved me, never told me he was proud of me, never even hugged me. The only thing I had left from my dad was an old tackle box and silence.

The tears suddenly turned to anger. I was angry at my father, angry at myself, angry at God. And I remember crying out to God, "This is it? This is all I get? I don't even have my father's signature!"

Left with Nothing

It was a crazy thing to say at the moment. But for some silly reason that only God knew, I was suddenly desperate for something written from my dad. Something personal. Something to hold on to. And his signature is what came to mind.

Then God suddenly spoke to me. "Hey big shot, got a question for you," He said. "If you were to die today, what would be in the tackle box of your life? What would your children hold in their hands tomorrow that would let them know they were the treasures of your life?"

"Well, God," I admitted, "I guess nothing. Just like my father left me nothing."

I went to bed that night feeling sorry for myself. Didn't sleep much. I kept thinking about how my kids would remember me. I was sure they knew I loved them. Unlike my dad, I had told my children countless times that I loved them and was proud of them. But something within me said that wasn't enough. I needed to do more. I needed to give them something tangible that they could keep long after I was gone.

"I Need to Leave My Kids a Blessing!"

The thought just popped into my head. I didn't have a clue where it came from or what it meant, but it sounded good. A blessing? Yeah, all right, that sounded like something my kids might want. But what exactly was it, and how did you give it to others? Was it like giving them a cold? Did you just stand back and sneeze your blessings all over them? I didn't know.

I remembered a book I'd once read about the importance of giving and receiving a blessing. It was appropriately called *The Blessing*, and it was by two of my favorite authors, Gary Smalley and John Trent. Aha! Maybe that's where the idea had come from! Convinced that the secret to giving a blessing lay within that book's hallowed pages, I leaped from my bed and proceeded to tear the house apart looking for it everywhere—except the bookcase. (I mean, who keeps books in a bookcase, right?)

Two hours later, with the contents of nightstands, closets, and shelves cluttering every room in the house, I finally found it—in the bookcase. I stayed up all night rereading the entire book. It felt like manna from heaven. There in those pages was the secret of the blessing in all its glory. Simply put, to bestow a blessing upon your children meant you expressed to them your love and pride. But the book also offered a word of caution. Giving a blessing wasn't to be taken lightly. It was serious stuff. The authors plainly stated that it was the greatest gift a father could give his children, one that could profoundly affect the rest of their lives.

Of course, I still didn't have a clue how to offer this blessing. But I did know I wanted my kids to remember me for more than an old tackle box. So I swore right then and there that I would bless my children. Still, telling them verbally seemed redundant. I'd done that their whole lives. No, I wanted to leave something behind. Something permanent.

And that brought me to the idea of writing a letter. If one letter was good, then two had to be better. And then three and four and five. That's it! I'd write them letters for the rest of my life! So many letters it would take them the rest of their lives just to read them all! They would be poignant letters, filled with what was important to me and why I loved them, and about my hopes and dreams and wishes for them—tons and tons of letters.

But where to start?

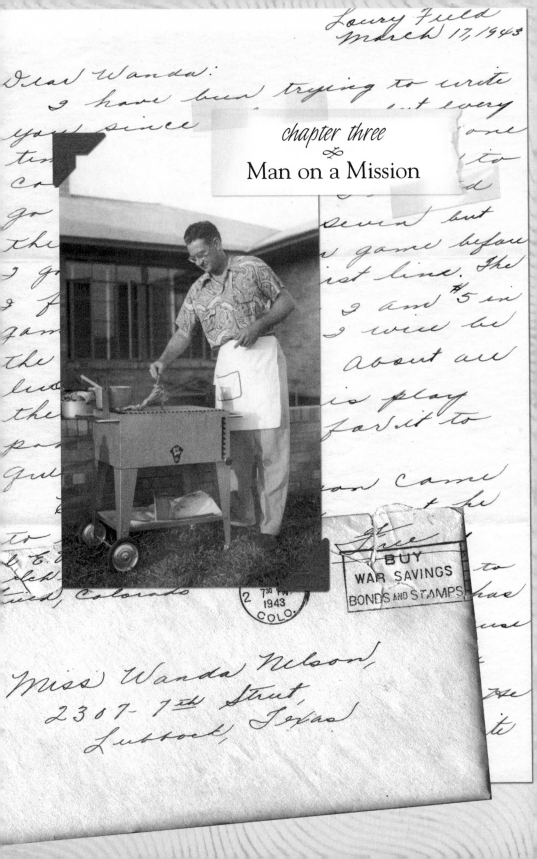

Loury Field
March 17, 1943

Dear Wanda:
    I have been trying to write
you since   ...t every
ten   ...one
co   ...to
go   ...d
the   seven but
I g   game before
I f   rst line. The
fam   I am #5 in
the   I will be
lue   about all
the   is play
pa   for it to
gue   ...came
to   ...t he
...   ...
..., Colorado

chapter three
&
Man on a Mission

miss Wanda Nelson,
2307- 7th Strut,
Lubbock, Texas

BUY
WAR SAVINGS
BONDS AND STAMPS

We were just going to get together and do what men do best—eat—and then see if we couldn't figure this thing out.

*I*f you're going to write a letter, you need stationery, right? And if you're talking about writing to your kids, it should be the finest stationery you can find! So the next morning, I went straight to the best stationery store I knew of and told the salesman I wanted the most expensive stationery he had, and I wanted the nicest, most expensive leather binder so I would have some place to keep those letters once I'd written them, and I wanted those binders embossed and engraved with the names of my kids . . . and . . . and . . . puff! puff! gasp! gasp! . . . I was so excited I was hyperventilating.

I bent over to put my head between my knees while asking, "How much?"

"Hundred dollars each," smiled the salesman, sensing a big sale.

"Great," I gasped. "I'll take seven."

"Seven?!?" The salesman's jaw hit the floor. This wasn't a sale. This was the beginning of a college education for his kids. "What in the world are you doing?" he asked.

"I'm going on an adventure," I smiled proudly, straightening up, "to bless my children."

He was so amazed he brought out the other employees and asked me to tell them what I was doing. I'll never forget the response of two young men who came out from working in the back. When they heard what I was doing, they looked at each other with amazement. "My dad would never do that!" one of them said.

Yep. That's me. Super Dad.

The Adventure Begins

Of course, one man's adventure is another man's folly—especially when his wife's the one who pays the bills and knows his credit card balance. You see, money is in short supply around our house. I've had to learn a difficult lesson in physics since having children. You've heard of Newton's Third Law of Motion?

For every action, there is an equal and opposite reaction.

Well, for a father with seven kids that should read: for every kid you have, there is an equal and opposite drop in spendable income.

That's right, I have seven kids. No, I'm not a rabbit. They're not all mine. Well, four are. The other three are from my wife's first marriage. But the bottom line is, Carolyn and I have always felt like they're all ours. Consequently, we have ten cars in the driveway, five kids in college, and an empty bank account. We're living proof of the father's version of Newton's law at work.

You Did What?!?

So spending seven hundred dollars on stationery gave my wife cause to pause. I secretly hoped she wasn't using that time to find something heavy to throw at me, but either way it didn't matter. I was determined I was going to bless my kids. The sins of the fathers were going to stop with me.

"But you can't write," she said as kindly as she could.

"Yes, I can," I protested weakly.

"No. You can't."

Determined to prove her wrong, I grabbed my fancy new stationery and my forty-dollar pen (Oops! Forgot to tell you about that!) and sat down to write my letters. And that's when I discovered something.

My wife was right.

Don't you just hate that? Did I mention I made C's and D's in English? I couldn't construct sentences on paper back then, and nothing had changed. I wasn't a writer! What was I thinking? After spending all that money on stationery and binders and pens, I was still as lost as a blind miner.

Avoiding my wife's knowing look, I immediately went back to reading *The Blessing*. Good stuff. Filled with the importance of bestowing a blessing, but unfortunately not much on the old "shoe leather, one, two, three...here's how you do it" approach.

Gathering the Twelve

So what's a grammatically challenged, middle-aged man to do? Call his friends, of course. Twelve names immediately came to mind. Men I knew who loved their kids and might want to learn how to bless them. When I told them what I was doing, they all asked the same thing.

"Is this a Bible study?"

No. We were just going to get together and do what men do best—eat—and then see if we couldn't figure this thing out. They all said yes. Every one of them. Now that's friendship. Or was it the free lunch? Hmmm . . . no, I think it was the friendship. And the fact that these guys truly loved their kids and giving them a blessing sounded like a great idea.

Little did we know what an amazing adventure lay before us.

chapter four

The Dirty Dozen . . .
Plus Two

Mission Statement:
To leave a legacy of faith,
hope, and love to our children
and our children's children.

I couldn't have been more shocked. I invited twelve men to lunch and fourteen showed up. No, I wasn't upset; I was excited. It meant I wasn't alone. There were a lot of guys like me—guys who loved their kids and wanted to bless them but didn't know how.

Now what? They naturally assumed I had a plan. (I knew there was something I forgot!) So I started with the easy thing: lunch. And while we ate, I asked the men to go around the table and introduce themselves since some of them didn't know each other.

"And when you describe yourself," I said, "include three things about yourself: your wife's name, how many kids you have, and why you're here."

Each of them rattled off quick answers to the first two questions, but when it came to why they had come they all said the same thing: "Because you asked me!"

OK, fine. That was a start. Whatever journey lay ahead (and somehow I sensed it was going to be a long one), I couldn't have twelve, um, fourteen men with whom I'd rather be traveling. After all, a single strand of rope is strong, but several strands together are unbreakable. There is great power in a group of like-minded Christian men seeking God's will.

Who were these men? Let me introduce you to three of them. No, better yet, let them introduce themselves . . .

My Fellow Travelers

"Hi, my name's Jim Canton, and I really don't want to be here. In fact, when Greg originally asked me to come, I told him no. The whole idea of writing a letter of blessing to my children was just too painful. You see, I got divorced eight years ago. The experience was extremely bitter, and my kids ended up siding with my wife. My wife went on to marry a very wealthy man, and he forbade my kids from ever having contact with me. He told them that if they did, he would cut them off. But to be honest, he didn't have to tell them that. They were still too angry and upset by the divorce to speak with me. Bottom line: I haven't spoken with my kids in five years. Five years. So when Greg challenged me to be a part of the group, I told him I just couldn't. I couldn't bear the thought of writing to my kids, of putting my heart and soul into a letter, only to be rejected. But then Greg said an interesting thing. He said, 'Jim, since when are you responsible for how they respond? Your sole responsibility is to communicate your love and blessing to your children. Nothing more.' After hearing those words over and over again in my mind and praying about it, I called Greg and told him I'd come. Do I want to be here? No. Do I need to be here? Absolutely."

"Hi, my name is Dirk Howard, and my story's not nearly as dramatic as Jim's. When Greg called me and asked me if I'd come, I immediately said yes. I'd love to learn how to write a letter of blessing to my kids. I have no such letter from my dad; but I do have a letter. One I treasure. I've carried it around in my briefcase for twenty years. If you read it, you'd probably wonder why. My dad was a farmer and the letter just talks about a day in his life. He talks about the cows that need feeding and the fences that need mending. Nothing anyone in their right mind would ever consider important—certainly not important enough that someone would carry it around for years. So why have I? Because it's all that I have of my dad. I have three children: two teens and a ten-year-old whom I adore. And I can think of nothing I would love more than to learn how to write a letter of blessing to them. And maybe, if I'm lucky, they'll still be carrying it around long after I'm gone. I'd like that."

"Hi, my name is Jose Martinez and I came to Christ four years ago. You couldn't find a worse example of a father. I ran an airline and I was never around while my children were growing up. Then I scandalized my family by getting caught in multiple affairs. My wife and I finally divorced, and I lost everything—my marriage, my children, everything that was important to me. And yet, in the midst of all that, I found Christ. He radically changed my life. I'm now a new man, and by God's grace, I'm trying to put my life back together. I would love to learn how to write a letter of blessing to my children because I would like to think that somehow God will use it to help me communicate to my family my deep sorrow and regret over my past behavior, and to let them know that because of Jesus Christ I'm a new man."

Faith, Hope, and Love

There wasn't a man in the group who hadn't been through some serious challenges in his life. And although our stated goal was to bless our children, I think we all could have used a little blessing ourselves. That was my prayer as we began that first meeting; that God would use these letters to bless both the sender and the receiver.

Once everyone had introduced themselves, it was time to get to work. Of course, being businessmen, we decided we needed to first come up with a mission statement for our group, guidelines for what would be our focus.

As a group, we decided our mandate would be Malachi 4:6: "He will turn the hearts of the fathers to their children, and the hearts of the children to their fathers."

Why did we choose this verse? Because it's a command from God. Check out Psalm 78:1-7:

"O my people, hear my teaching; listen to the words of my mouth. I will open my mouth in parables, I will utter hidden things, things from of old—what we have heard and known, what our fathers have told us. We will not hide them from their children; we will tell the next generation the praiseworthy deeds of the LORD, his power, and the wonders he has done. He decreed statutes for Jacob and established the law in Israel, which he commanded our forefathers to teach their children, so the next generation would know them, even the children yet to be born, and they in turn would tell their children. Then they would put their trust in God and would not forget his deeds but would keep his commands."

God's not asking us to do this; He's telling us to. Armed with a scriptural mandate, the group came up with a mission statement: to leave a legacy of faith, hope, and love to our children and our children's children.

I then told the men about Smalley and Trent's book, *The Blessing*, and passed out copies. While they thumbed quizzically through the pages, I told them I wanted us to use this book as a template for discovering how to bless our kids. But of course the most important book we'd rely upon would be the Bible.

"It's got to be filled with tons of stuff on giving blessings," I volunteered.

For once I was right.

*A blessing is the unmerited,
undeserved favor of God.*

$\mathcal{A}$s we dug into our Bibles, we found the Lord had a lot to say on the subject. The first thing we discovered was that there are three types of blessings:

1. General Blessings We All Receive—When you woke up this morning and your heart was beating, you experienced a blessing from God. Every sunrise and sunset are blessings from God. They are equal-opportunity blessings, available to everyone.

2. Blessings of God that Christians Experience—These are blessings that are specific to believers who enter into a relationship with Jesus Christ. Among them are the joy and peace that only Christians can experience when they've placed their faith in the Lord.

3. Blessings We Give to Others—In human terms, this can be any blessing that you bestow upon another, both tangible and intangible. When you give to the Salvation Army, you're imparting a blessing on someone. But you also give a blessing when you tell your son, "I'm so proud of you!"

So how does God define a blessing? Again, Scripture has the answer.

A blessing is the unmerited, undeserved favor of God. Proverbs 10:22 says, "The blessing of the LORD brings wealth, and he adds no trouble to it."

That's not just talking about monetary blessing. That refers to what makes our lives truly rich: family, love, health, happiness. The important things.

Such a blessing brings with it four principles:

PRINCIPLE ONE: Ask for God's Blessing—In 2 Timothy 1:2-3, Paul writes, "To Timothy, my dear son: Grace, mercy and peace from God the Father and Christ Jesus our Lord. I thank God, whom I serve, as my forefathers did, with a clear conscience, as night and day I constantly remember you in my prayers."

Paul was petitioning God day and night on Timothy's behalf, asking God to bless Timothy with grace, mercy, and peace. Wow! We could all use a friend like that. So how do we ask God for His blessing? By asking for His favor, by asking for His power, and by asking for His protection.

God doesn't want you to be timid. He loves it when you ask. Paul basically starts his letter by writing, "How I thank God for you, Timothy."

Let's try a little exercise. Try substituting one of your children's names for Timothy's. Go ahead, try it.

"How I thank God for you, _____. I pray for you every night and day. I pray God will bless you with grace, mercy, and peace."

Isn't that great? You're asking for God's favor in your child's life! And while you're at it, don't forget to also ask for His power. His supernatural power. We're not talking wimpy stuff here. We're talking God's power! Just think, God wants to bestow that power on those you pray for and those you bless in your life.

God also wants you to pray for His protection over your loved ones. What father doesn't worry when his child is out late at night or heading off to college for the first time? What can you do? Pray for God's protecting hand to be over them.

PRINCIPLE TWO: Recognize God's Blessing—For most of us, this requires some learning. We're not always accustomed to seeing God's blessings and acknowledging that they're from Him. This requires cultivating a thankful heart and developing a spirit of appreciation for what we already have. When it comes to your children, the key verse to remember is Psalm 127:3: "Sons are a heritage from the LORD, children a reward from him."

It's taken me forty years to learn to recognize God's blessings. I had to learn to put on my spiritual eyeglasses so that I could see all the things God has done for me. Of course, like most things in my Christian life, it remains a work in progress, but I do try to begin each day with a renewed appreciation for the blessings God has given me. "Thank You, Lord, for a wife who loves me, for the food in my pantry, and for the kids upstairs who aren't sick or hurting."

Next time you get up in the morning and walk outside to pick up the paper, notice that the sun is shining and the birds are singing, and try saying a quick, "Thank You, Lord!"

Do this every day and you will change. You can't help it.

PRINCIPLE THREE: Receive God's Blessing—It's crazy that we have to be told to accept God's blessing, but doing so requires more than just saying, "OK, Lord, sock it to me!" There are three prerequisites:

1. You must fear/revere the Lord. Proverbs 1:7 says, "The fear of the LORD is the beginning of knowledge." This means you recognize God is in control of your life and that without Him, you can do nothing.

2. You must trust God. Proverbs 3:5-6 says, "Trust in the LORD with all your heart and lean not on your own under-

31

standing; in all your ways acknowledge him, and he will make your paths straight." In other words, when you're praying for guidance and you've done everything you're supposed to— you've acknowledged that God's in control and you aren't— then you can trust that what the Lord shows you to do is truly the best thing for you.

3. You must obey God. Ouch! That's the tough one, isn't it? Why is it so hard? Because it requires sacrifice and submission. In our finite view of the world, we can't possibly know what's best for us. Want to stay out of trouble? Just obey God.

PRINCIPLE FOUR: Give Blessings to Others—The key verse to remember here is Malachi 3:10: "'Bring the whole tithe into the storehouse, that there may be food in my house. Test me in this,' says the LORD Almighty, 'and see if I will not throw open the floodgates of heaven and pour out so much blessing that you will not have room enough for it.'" In other words, pass it on, giving of your time, your talent, and your money. And when you do, God will bless you abundantly with the things that matter.

POST CARD

ADDRESS

STAMP

RMS

OGDEN R.P.O.

JUL 23 1942

Will write
when get
to Salt
Lake.
Earl

Miss Wanda Nelson,
Matador, Texas
Box # 566.

Published by Carpenter Paper Co., Salt Lake City.

B B
Barkalow Bros. Publishers
Omaha, Neb.

*Like Don Quixote in search
of windmills, we set off
into the unknown.*

*A*rmed with all this brand new knowledge about blessings, the group and I were now ready to take the next step. It was time to bless our kids!

I commissioned the men to do the same thing I had done: go find some stationery, a leather binder, and a box. Why a box? Because I'd decided to use the leather binders for duplicate copies of our letters (in case someone lost one) and give the recipients a nice wooden box that would be a safe haven for their letters. But not just any nice wooden box would do. No sir, not for our kids! It had to be large enough to hold lots of letters, and it had to be made of polished mahogany with a brass plate on the front engraved with the child's name. I thought about having it overlaid with gold, but since I'd have to hock my house to pay for seven of them, I quickly dropped the idea. And what would we call such a box? We'd call it . . .

A Memory Box

Nice, huh? I thought so too. But some of the men were looking confused.

"What do you mean, 'large enough to hold lots of letters'? You mean we're writing more than one?"

"Yep. We're going to write tons of letters for the rest of our lives. And you should title them so they can be distinguished from each other."

As soon as I mentioned we were going to be writing letters for the rest of our lives, a corporate GULP! went up from the group. They hadn't planned on this being a lifetime commitment. The troops were wavering. Time for some encouragement.

"Did you know if you only wrote three letters a year to your kids and the Lord lets you live another twenty years, you will have written them an entire book by the time you die?"

Amazement circled that room like the wave at a football stadium.

"Wow, only three a year?"

"Yep."

"I can do that!"

I had them against the ropes. Time to go for the knockout punch.

"And after we write our kids, what do you say we write our parents? Oh, and you know what else we could do? We could write a final letter to our families—sort of the last letter of our lives."

They came off the ropes swinging.

"But I already have a will!"

"I'm not talking about a will . . . well, maybe I am, but it's a different kind of will. This is one that tells your loved ones about the spiritual possessions you want to leave them—your hopes and dreams and desires for their lives."

The men paused to think about that. They seemed to like the idea. So it was time to drop the other shoe.

"Oh yeah . . . of course that means we're going to have to meet a few extra times."

"How many extra times?"

"Well, three. Once to talk about our letters to our kids, once to talk about the ones to our parents, and then a final meeting for our final letter."

There were a lot of concerned looks. These were busy men. The last thing they needed was one more commitment. But guess what? They all agreed. God was at work.

"OK, great. So by the time we get together again, we'll have written letters to our kids, right?"

Clint Reynolds, one of my best friends, raised his hand and said, "I can't do that."

"Why can't you?" I asked. "I know you love your kids."

"No, you don't understand," he replied. "I can't write a letter to my kids unless I first write one to my wife. She's the one who gave me the privilege of being called a dad."

Now it was time for me to gulp! Of course we had to write letters to our wives! Why didn't I think of that?

"OK, we're writing four letters."

That meant we now had to meet four more times. That's five meetings total. It was a big commitment for these guys, but there were no complaints. On the contrary, the men were genuinely excited. We decided that by the time we got together for our next meeting, we would have written our letters to our wives and delivered them.

Of course, that threw us into a panic because we still didn't have a clue how to do that. Common sense told us there were two things a letter to our wives shouldn't be:

1. Long—we're men for goodness sake! Most of us couldn't hold a thought longer than two seconds. So we settled on a letter of no more than one page in length.

2. And it shouldn't be correctional—not unless we wanted our wives to write back! Seriously, the goal of our letter should be to communicate our unconditional love and blessing. Period. Nothing more.

We then came up with a plan for delivering this letter. We were to take our wives out to dinner, on no special occasion, and without her knowledge, give the box containing our letter to the restaurant's maitre d' for safekeeping. After dessert, we would retrieve the box and present it to our wives.

The men committed to do this, and we all went our separate ways with a lot of fear and trepidation. Why such worry? Because we didn't know how our wives would respond. Laughter, scorn, ridicule, apathy—all were possible. Some of the men's marriages were a bit rocky. And even for the ones that weren't, this was definitely out of character for most of us. But we were committed to following God's will regardless, so like Don Quixote in search of windmills, we set off into the unknown.

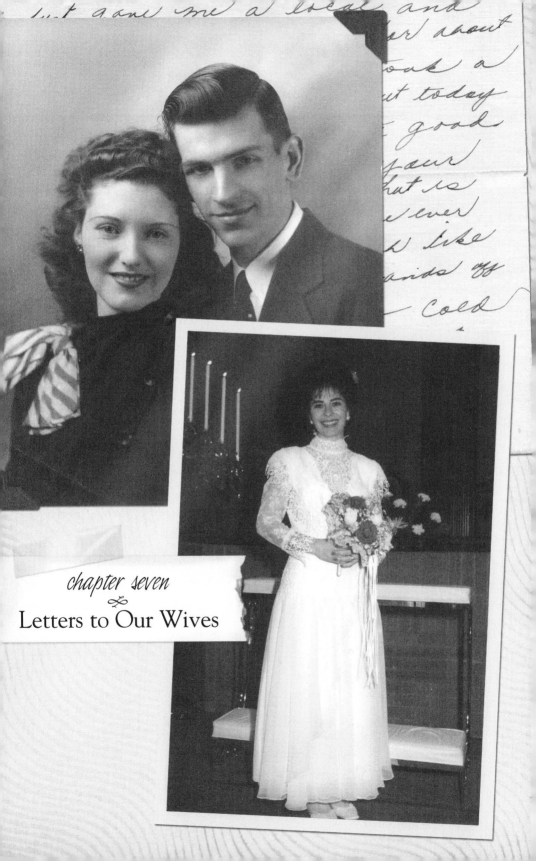

...t gave me a local and
...er about
...ok a
...t today
...good
...your
...hat is
...ever
...like
...ands off
...cold

chapter seven

Letters to Our Wives

Where does such love come from?

*L*ittle by little, what happened over the next month began to filter back to me. The men had done as assigned. They'd written letters to their wives and delivered them. But being typical guys, there were some glitches. Some guys had used mismatched stationery—some striped, some green, some orange—and some of them couldn't find the boxes I'd recommended, so they just used any old box!

Even writing the letters proved more challenging than expected. Some men found themselves staring at their computer screens, while others couldn't help but weep as they wrote.

One of the guys said, "It was like a volcano exploding because I was tapping into a side of me I'd never tapped into before."

Other men said that as soon as they started working on their letters, they started fighting with their wives, fussing and arguing like they hadn't done in years.

Was this a disaster in the making?

No, it was to be expected. After all, whenever you attempt to do something like this, you open yourself up to spiritual warfare. Especially when you're talking about marriage. God's not the only one who has a plan for your marriage.

God's plan says, THE TWO SHALL BECOME ONE.

Satan's plan says, THE ONE SHALL BECOME TWO.

Why does Satan hate Christian marriages so much? Because they are a mirror of Christ's relationship with believers.

Paul writes in Ephesians 5:25: "Husbands, love your wives, just as Christ loved the church and gave himself up for her." And just to make sure we got the point, Paul goes on to write in verse 32, "This is a profound mystery—but I am talking about Christ and the church." A Christian marriage is a witness to the world. When nonbelievers see us loving, honoring, respecting, supporting, and encouraging our wives, they stare in wonder. And they can't help but ask, "Where does such love come from?"

An Imprint That Will Never Wash Away

Despite the arguments, tears, fears, and tacky stationery, the men had persevered. It would take a lot more than a little spiritual warfare to stop these guys. They wrote their letters and delivered them with mixed feelings of excitement and anxiety. Then they held their breath. What happened next?

"It was the best thing that's happened in twenty-five years of marriage!"

It was my good friend, Ken Rondale, speaking. The team had gotten together for our second lunch meeting to debrief.

"I'm sorry, Ken, what did you say?" I asked.

"I said it was the best thing that's happened in twenty-five years of marriage!"

"But what about the green-striped stationery in the tacky box?"

"Oh that," frowned Ken. "Yeah, my wife thought that was pretty funny. But after she read the letter, she said she wouldn't have cared if I'd written it on orange toilet paper and stuffed it in a sock. I know we weren't supposed to give our letters to our wives on a special occasion, but it was our anniversary, and our whole family came over to the house and . . . um, guess I messed up on that too! We were supposed to take them to a restaurant, weren't we? OK, I guess I broke all the rules."

"That's alright," I said. "Those weren't rules; they were just guidelines. You have to do what works for you. So what happened next?"

"Well, like I said, our whole family was there—kids, parents, the works—and I had the box gift-wrapped really nice. When she opened it she got all teary, so I asked her if it was OK if I read it to the whole family, and that made her cry even harder, but she managed to croak out a "Yes!" So I read it to the family, and when I did, she felt really honored. She told me that was what she loved the most, that I'd publicly said those words to her in front of the family. Like I said, it was the best thing that's happened in twenty-five years of marriage."

Everyone clapped for Ken, then suddenly it was like a dam bursting. The stories kept coming and coming until they flooded the room.

"I ended up tearing up my first letter," said my friend Butch McArthur. "But my next one I liked pretty well. So I put it in my box, wrapped it up, and took my wife, Wendy, to dinner and gave it to her. I guess I did OK with the letter, because when she read it, she began to cry and she gave me a big kiss and thanked me profusely."

"My wife couldn't even get through my letter," said my buddy Larry Bradford. "She began to cry and asked me to read it, and when I did, we both started crying. There we were, sitting on the couch, bawling like babies. I cried so much I had to change my shirt."

"Guess I sorta messed up too," apologized one of the other men, Randy Candell, "because I didn't take my wife to a restaurant either."

"Where'd you take her?" I asked.

"Fancy hotel. Sneaked into our room before she got there and did a little decorating, so when she showed up, there were rose petals everywhere, and candlelight and champagne and chocolates . . . oh, and my box, beautifully wrapped, sitting on the bed. After she read my letter, she said it was the greatest treasure of her life."

Every story was like this. Story after story. Amazing stories. Every one different, and yet every one the same. The men had blessed their wives.

They admitted to being nervous, watching carefully as their wives read their letters. Some of the men were disappointed because their wives refused to read their letters publicly, afraid they might cry. But no matter what happened, they all agreed with Ken . . .

It was the greatest thing that had ever happened in their marriage!

Lowry Field, Colo
July 21, 1943

Dear Wanda:

I guess you are wondering what happened to the letter I was supposed to have written Sunday. I had planned that note we could get away Sundays. After day I just wrote even as work we carried and the Carbine, rifle and machine gun. It the rifles kicking like a mule machine gun was a lot of fun. I have some shots on my shoulder like legs.

Strong marriages had been made stronger, and marriages on the verge of collapse had begun to heal.

*O*ver and over again, as I listened to these men's stories, the same word kept coming out. Treasure. Their wives treasured their letters. They treasured the box it came in and the way it was given and, most of all, they treasured the man who had given it.

Isn't that a great word? Of course it brings to mind that cautionary verse: "For where your treasure is, there your heart will be also" (Matthew 6:21).

Yes sir, you can buy your wife a big house or an expensive car, but if you really want to show her how much you love her, get her a beautiful wooden box and put a letter in it telling her so.

A Treasure That Will Last an Eternity

I can hardly describe how excited I was as I listened to all these stories. Strong marriages had been made stronger, and marriages on the verge of collapse had begun to heal. Satan had to be one seriously unhappy camper.

But perhaps the most tender story of all came from my friend, Mark Foxworthy.

"I told my wife, Carol, I wanted her to go on a special dinner with me," said Mark. "It wasn't our anniversary, it wasn't her birthday . . . no special holiday or anything like that. So Carol was naturally a little suspicious. She kept asking me what was going on, but I wouldn't tell her. After we were seated in her favorite restaurant, I excused myself and went to the maitre d' and said, 'I need your help. I've got this box in a bag and I need you to keep it someplace safe until I come get it right after we have dessert.'

"OK, picture this. I've just told the man in charge of a

crowded public place in a large city in the United States that I had a box in a bag that I wanted him to hold on to. That's like Osama bin Laden asking you to hold his seat on a plane. The maitre d' gave me this look like, *My mama didn't raise no dumb children,* as he asked, 'May I ask what's in the box, sir?'

"'It's a letter telling my wife how much I love her,' I said. I opened the box and let him have a peek. For the first time he smiled, and the hostess next to him said, 'Oh, that's so sweet!' Then the maitre d' said with a twinkle in his eye, 'I would be honored to hold it for you, sir.'

"I went back to our table and my wife and I had a wonderful dinner. After dessert, I excused myself again and went back to the maitre d' and said, 'OK, now's the time.' He gave me my box and as I carried it back to my table, the maitre d', the hostess, and a lot of the other staff followed behind me, giggling like little kids. Of course, that got everyone in the restaurant staring. And I'll never forget my wife's face as she looked up and saw me approaching with this enormous entourage.

"'Why are you doing this?' she asked.

"'Just because I love you,' I said as I handed her the box.

"Of course that made the whole restaurant go, 'Ahhhh!!!!' How embarrassing. But after she opened the letter and read it, she looked up at me, tears in her eyes, and even though we were surrounded by strangers, it was like we were the only two people on earth.

"And then she said to me, 'To know that you took the time to do all this—to put your thoughts and words on paper, and to do so without fear, without shame, and without worrying what anyone else thought—I just want you to know from my heart, I will treasure this forever. You have made an imprint on my life that will never wash away.'"

Wow.

No, let me rephrase that . . . WOW!!!

Mark did good, didn't he? I wish I could tell you about all the other stories that came from the group, but they would all fill a book on their own. Suffice to say, the reaction of the men's wives was so far beyond our wildest expectations that we could hardly wait to start writing letters to our kids!

THIS SPACE FOR MESSA

Published by Carpenter Paper Co., Salt Lake City, Utah

BUT SEE AMERICA FIRST

Cedar
Southern Utah. This
of the many marvel
mations in this distr
a trip through Cedar
by those visiting Br
Zion's Canyon should
omitted.

Barstow Bros. Publishers
Omaha·Neb

chapter nine

Letters to Our Children

*I love you and I want
to know what's important
in your life. Tell me how I
can be an encouragement.*

$\mathcal{W}$e'd finally gotten there—our third meeting. Time to write a letter to our kids.

A letter from Dad.

Since we'd be writing lots of letters, it would actually be . . . LETTERS FROM DAD.

Hence the title of this book. Of course when this title came to me, I wasn't thinking about writing a book. I was just getting together with fourteen of my best friends to have lunch and try to figure out how to bless those we loved. It wasn't a ministry. It wasn't even a Bible study. But still, I thought, it would be nice to have something to call our little lunch group, in case someone asked.

So Letters From Dad was born.

Who's Your Daddy?

We hear that a lot, don't we? "Who's your daddy?" It's sort of the hip thing to say. Late-night television especially loves it. Jay Leno will yell, "Who's your daddy?" and everyone will laugh. But I've got news for you, guys. The joke's on us. There are a lot of children out there who don't know who their daddy is. And I'm not just talking about children who've lost their fathers; I'm talking about children who actually have a father, but he's never around.

That's sad, not only for the child, but for the father who has no idea what he's missing.

One of my favorite proverbs says "Children's children are a crown to the aged" (Proverbs 17:6).

Boy, can I identify with that! I've just become a grandfather for the first time. I could've never in my wildest dreams imagined myself a grandfather. I mean, I just got used to being a dad! But that first time I held my grandbaby . . . oh, man! Do you know that feeling? It's just like that "new daddy rush" you got when they handed you your firstborn, like a wave washing over you, transforming you by the hand of God from a selfish human being into one of total sacrifice. In that instant you would give your life for your child—no questions asked, no regrets.

That same old feeling came rushing back when I held my grandbaby for the first time.

But there's a second part to Proverbs 17:6: "and parents are the pride of their children."

When I read that verse for the first time, it drove me to my knees. The pride of my children . . . is me? I don't know how that makes you feel, but it gives me the heebie-jeebies. Am I worthy of their pride? Often not. That leaves me with two choices: surrender my God-given responsibility as a dad and leave my children for others to raise; or accept that responsibility and go to battle for my kids.

And believe me, it's a battle. There are a lot of people out there more than willing to raise your kids for you. No, it's not a secret organization of evil nannies. It's your kids' friends, their teachers, advertisers who want to sell them something, even rock stars and movie stars who want to convert your children to their way of life. There's any number of people willing to fill the vacuum of an absentee parent.

As for me, I choose to be the dad, warts and all. I choose to make a commitment to my children to always be there. I choose to be involved in their lives. I choose to give them guidance and expect obedience. They don't always like it, but hey, I'm the dad. I'm on a mission from God and I take that very seriously. Yes, I make mistakes. Oh boy, do I! I've fallen on my face so many times my nose has a permanent upturn. But every time I do, I pick myself up, dust myself off, straighten my nose, and go at it again. And though I may not be perfect, I've yet to see a child who didn't respond to a father who loves him. And I do love my kids. More than life itself.

How can I demonstrate that love? In lots of ways. But one really good way is to write them a letter of blessing.

On Your Mark, Get Set, Write!

At the previous meeting of our Letters From Dad lunch group, we had talked about the impact of our letters on our wives and the joy those letters brought to both the giver and the receiver. Now that it was time to write our kids, I opened our third meeting by asking the men three questions.

1. Is there anything you wish you could say to your kids but have never said?

When it comes to life, we're all merely tenants, and there

are no long-term leases. Remember *carpe diem*, the Latin phrase that was all the rage for a while? Why did "seize the day" strike such a chord with people? Because we all know that none of us is guaranteed a tomorrow. Interestingly, even Scripture encourages us to do the same thing. Remember what the Lord said in Matthew 6:34? "Therefore do not worry about tomorrow, for tomorrow will worry about itself. Each day has enough trouble of its own."

If you are to live each day as if there's no tomorrow, then it might be a good idea to say whatever it is that needs to be said. If you've never told your kids you love them, don't wait. Tell them. If you've never told your kids you're proud of them, tell them. Do it now. Not tomorrow. Not after they've done something special. Right now. Are your kids around? Can you reach them by phone? Then what are you waiting for? Lay this book down and go tell them. All you have to say is, "I love you so much and I am so proud of you."

Is that really so hard? Sure, it might be risky. You may even get questioned or laughed at. Heaven forbid they don't respond like you want. But do it anyway. Be a blessing kamikaze: strike without warning and risk it all.

But if you've said things to your kids you regret, then some kind of reparation needs to be made. And as the man of the house, the spiritual leader (whether you've actually acted like this or not), it's up to you to take the first step. Apologize. Do it this very moment. Don't wait. You may never have another chance.

2. Is there anything you wish you'd taught your kids but have never done so?

Remember Proverbs 22:6? "Train a child in the way he should go, and when he is old he will not turn from it." Before

I was a father, I dreamed of teaching my kids to ride bikes and play baseball. But after I became a father, I realized the most important thing I could teach my kids was to love, respect, and fear the Lord. The most important life lessons are those that lead from your heart to your child's heart to God's heart.

3. Do you possess a letter of love, blessing, and affirmation from your father?

You know my story. I don't possess such a letter. I don't even have my father's signature. How I wish I did.

How about you? Do you possess such a letter? If you do, praise the Lord! Count yourself blessed. Now pass on that blessing to your children. But if you're like me, if you possess no such letter, then declare before the Lord that this will end with you. Don't let another day go by without writing your children and giving them your blessing.

But Where Do I Start?

Same place I started. Sit down and think about your children—their fears, concerns, dreams, anything that's important to them. If you don't know what these things are, find out. Do it one-on-one, not just with an e-mail or a phone call. Take them to lunch, dinner, any place you can be alone, and then say to them, "I love you and I want to know what's important in your life. Tell me how I can be an encouragement in your life."

Make a list of these things. It will become the table of contents for all your future letters.

Take marriage, for example. Everyone faces the prospect at some point in his or her life. If your child is concerned about marriage, put it in your table of contents and send your child a letter on the subject. And don't just advise what not to do. Talk about the positive things, especially God's plan as it relates to marriage. Mention your own hopes and dreams for their future married life.

Of course, if your children are still young, their concerns will reflect their age. Peer pressure, dating, and sex are all things teenagers face. But even really young kids have to deal with death, divorce, and separation. So be a student of your children, ferret out all these things, and then write them a letter.

And do it *now*.

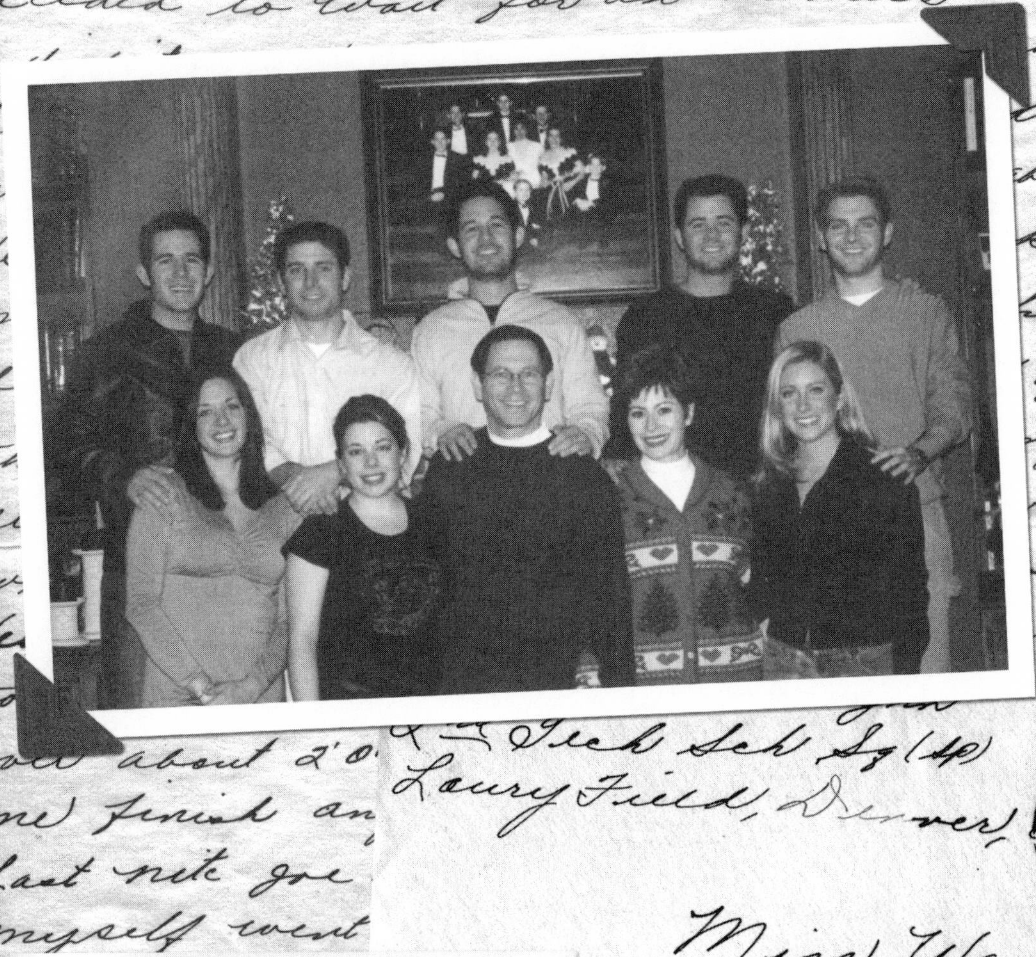

chapter ten

Words of Faith, Hope, and Love

*Faith, hope, and love will
never go out of style.*

$\mathcal{N}$ eed help with your table of contents? The following is what I came up with for my own kids:

Letters From Dad
Words of Faith, Hope, and Love
Table of Contents
The Blessing Box & Letter (Christmas 2002)

I showed this table of contents to the men in my lunch group, then encouraged them to come up with their own. This got us into a discussion of what was worthy to be included. The answer? If it's important to your child, it's worthy. Notice I said "if it's important to your child." We're not talking about you here. Sorry, guys, but your kids might come up with things you think are really dumb. Doesn't matter. If it's important to them, then write them a letter treating that subject with respect and importance.

Of course, the converse is also true. As a father with a lot more life experience under my ever-expanding belt, God has shown me things that are important for my children to know. My children may not consider them important, but I'm obligated to put them in my table of contents anyway. And if they complain, I simply point to Psalm 78:1-7. Teaching them about God's plan for their life isn't an option; it's a command.

One of the items in your table of contents might simply be "Tough Choices." By way of example, I shared with the men in my group a phone call I'd received recently from my son. Trevor had been facing a tough decision at school, and I'd written him a letter offering encouragement a few weeks before.

Tough Choices

"Hey Dad, just wanted to tell you I got your letter." Trevor was calling me from school. I loved hearing his voice. He was always so upbeat. "And I wanted to say thanks. I was really at a loss about what to do, and when I got your letter, I found a quiet place to read it. Let me tell you, Dad, I was blown away by the wisdom, love, and grace that you put in it. Thanks. I don't mind telling you I shed a few tears, but I now know what I should do, and I'm really at peace about it. I can't tell you how much it helped hearing from you. And I have to tell you, you may think you wrote that letter, but the truth? It was really written by the hand of God."

He was right, of course. I told you I can't write. So if anything good ever comes from my pen, there's no doubt who's guiding it. Oh, and while we're telling stories, let me tell you another. I love this story! But then I would; it's from my daughter Becky.

The Greatest Gift

"Before my dad started writing us letters, my most precious keepsake from him was a wire hanger. He—for some crazy reason I don't know why—was in my closet one day when I was a little girl, and he took out a wire hanger, the kind that has the paper on it, and wrote, 'Becky, I love you, Dad.' Well, I kept it, and it's been hanging in my closet for about thirteen years. It's been with me through four years of college and various moves, and even after the paper turned yellow. Now it's come home and it's still hanging in my closet. As much as I love that hanger, I love my letters more. Daughters have this incredible longing to be blessed and loved by their father, and to read that love in a letter from my dad, it's the greatest gift a father could ever give."

Did you catch that? "It's the greatest gift a father could ever give." My sweet Becky said that. It didn't matter to her if my love came in the form of a wire hanger or a letter; she cherished it because it was from me. Wow. You should see the smudges on the page as I write this. They're from my tears.

Marching Orders

The guys now had their next assignment. They were to go home and start a table of contents, then get to writing. Notice I said "start their table of contents." It's important to understand that this list will be dynamic and ever-changing as your kids grow up. What's important to a three-year-old isn't nearly as important to a thirty-year-old. But what will never change is their need for faith, hope, and love in their lives. That will never go out of style.

And you can be the author of that.

A139. Cedar Breaks from Sunset View Point, Southern Utah

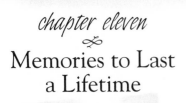

chapter eleven
❧
Memories to Last
a Lifetime

All past hurts were forgiven and forgotten.

*A*fter I sent the men home to begin writing their letters, I got a call from a man who'd heard about what we were doing. He said his church had a men's retreat coming up. They were thinking about having a father/daughter spaghetti dinner one of the nights and he wanted to know if I'd come speak.

"Absolutely," I said, "but under one condition. I want every one of the men to first write an 'I am blessed because . . .' letter to their daughter."

"What's that?" he asked.

"It's a letter that gives the many reasons why a dad is blessed to have his daughter as his precious child. And I want the fathers to read their letters to their daughters at the banquet."

He told the men about my request, and they readily agreed. In fact, they even made it a rule: you had to have your letter written, framed, and ready to deliver to your daughter the night of the banquet, or you couldn't get in.

When I showed up early to the banquet, the men were all there, cooking and decorating. They'd been at it all day. Of course, being typical guys, there was spaghetti sauce splashed everywhere, the smell of burnt toast in the air, red plastic table-cloths on the tables, along with plastic silverware and plastic grapes for a centerpiece. But those little girls couldn't care less.

You should've seen their eyes when they came in.

Sparkling. Like sparklers on the Fourth of July.

And I shouldn't say "little girls" because they ranged in age from five to thirty-five. But as all of us fathers know, once your little girl, always your little girl.

I started off by addressing the daughters: "Ladies, you will remember this night for as long as you live. It's a memory that will last a lifetime."

Then I turned to their fathers: "All right, gentlemen, it's time. Please present your daughters with your letters and read them."

For a moment nothing happened. Daughters stared at their fathers expectantly. Their fathers stared at the floor. It was pitiful. I've never seen so many nervous men. Men who could run corporations and make million-dollar deals were suddenly terrified.

But one by one I saw the daughters nudge their dads and smile their little-girl smiles, and one by one their fathers began to take out their letters. Then there was the scraping of chairs and the clearing of throats and the whispering of voices as the men began to read.

What an amazing sight! A bunch of big, old guys, shoulders hunched over, snuggled next to their little girls, reading their letters. And the tears? They were everywhere—in the love-filled eyes of the daughters and in the equally love-filled eyes of their fathers.

As I watched, I couldn't help thinking back to those wonderful times when my girls were young, snuggled in their beds, eyes sleepy, while I cuddled next to them reading of a bear named Pooh and the Hundred Acre Wood.

And I wept too.

At the end of the evening, after it was all over and everyone was leaving, I noticed a cute eight-year-old hugging her father as they walked out. As they passed me, the little girl whispered to her dad, "Daddy, this was the greatest night of my life."

Her father had given her a memory to last a lifetime. And

all because he took the time to entrust a few words to paper. Just a few.

So easy, so simple, and yet so profound.

Broken Hearts

I wish I could tell you that all the stories that came out of this time were as heartwarming. Unfortunately, they weren't. Several days after my spaghetti dinner, I began to hear back from the guys in my lunch group. Most of the stories were joyous—but not all. Some were heart-wrenching. Like what happened to my friend, Robin Benson.

I know of no one more passionate about leaving a legacy of faith, hope, and love to his kids than Robin Benson. Unfortunately, he'd been having problems with his teenage son. The teenage years are hard, but Robin saw this as an opportunity to encourage his son. So he wrote his son several letters—beautiful, treasured letters—written to bring about reconciliation, and he gave them to his son.

A few weeks later, his son returned and gave Robin the box back. "I don't want these," he said. And then he just walked away. When Robin looked inside the box, all he found were pieces of torn-up letters.

Another of the men I heard from is someone you've already met, Jim Canton. Remember him? He was the guy who had been through a difficult divorce and his ex-wife had remarried a wealthy man. Jim hadn't spoken to his kids in five years, but he was committed to giving it a try, in hopes his letters would bring about reconciliation. I can't tell you how he agonized over every word that filled those pages, apologizing for past wrongs and showering his kids with love and appreciation. Then, hands shaking, he'd gone to the mailbox and dropped in his letters. And then he waited . . . and he waited . . . and he waited . . . but the only response was silence.

Not one word from his kids.

And now Jim stood before me, a broken man. For all he knew, like Robin's son, they had torn them up.

The Moral of the Story

No one promised this would be easy. Just as there are no guarantees of tomorrow, there are no guarantees that those we wish to bless will want that blessing. So what are we to do? Bless them anyway. God calls on us to do so not out of expectation of return, but because He first blessed us.

Our response to rejection is to love unconditionally, just as our heavenly Father first loved us unconditionally.

Healed Hearts

Obviously, not all the stories were bad. As a matter of fact, one of the good ones was my own.

For a few months, my daughter Holley and I were at odds with one another. She's my oldest daughter and so precious to me. To have us not get along broke my heart. I decided I was going to write a letter giving her my love and blessing.

I thought and prayed about what to say. I even did a little research on the Internet. Then I sat down and wrote the letter. It took several drafts, but once I was happy with it, I asked Holley to meet with me. We found a nice, quiet place, just the two of us, and I began to read:

"You are my precious Holley. My firstborn. I'll never forget the time I found out your mother was pregnant and how I tricked her. She kept calling me, saying, 'Have you heard from the doctor?' And I'd say "no," but I'd heard from the doctor! I went out and bought a rocking cradle and put roses in it. When she came home, she couldn't believe it. That was such a joyous time. I remember often wondering what you'd be like. When I look at you today, you are everything I ever dreamed you'd be and more. You are my treasure. You are the precious one of my life. You're the one I love and would do anything for. When I look at you, my sweet Holley, I see those red highlights in your hair, and I see how unique God made you. You're a fiery little thing. God made you with fire in your bones. But He also made Peter with fire in his bones too. I've never, ever questioned how God made you. And I won't ever do that. I did some studying up on your name—Holley Ann Vaughn. Such a pretty name. Named after your grandmother. The name Vaughn means 'little man.' Appropriate, since I'm five-foot-seven and you're four-ten . . ."

" . . . and a half," said Holley, smiling.

"That's right," I said, returning that smile, " . . . and a half."

I continued reading.

"You may be small, but you're a powerhouse. Your middle name is Ann, which means "the gracious one." And you are gracious. You are gracious and kind, and I love to see you with other people, how you treat them so graciously. And your first name, Holley, means 'pure and holy one.' And so you are 'the pure and holy one, the gracious little person.' I picture for you a special future. For God will continue to make you like your name. He's got something so dynamic that He's going to do in your life. I don't know what it is. All I know is it's going to be exciting. But you need to know one thing: I am here for you and I am so committed to you. If you need me in the middle of the night, you know I'm there. Whatever it is, I'm there, until God takes me home. I am yours, you are mine, and I am your servant."

And then I asked Holley if I could pray for her. She said yes, so I prayed, "Father, take care of my little Holley. Make her into the woman You want her to be. Bless her, dear Jesus, keep her strong, make her to be like You. Make her to be gracious and kind and loving and pure and holy. In Jesus' name, amen."

By the time I finished that prayer, we were both crying. We hugged and then just sat there, holding one another. All past hurts forgiven and forgotten. Just a father and his daughter, loving each other.

Two hearts, healed.

chapter twelve
Letters to Our Parents

You gave me a tender heart
to love my children.

I opened the fourth meeting of our lunch group by reading from the Ten Commandments. In Exodus 20:12, God says, "Honor your father and your mother, so that you may live long in the land the LORD your God is giving you."

While studying this verse, I had discovered something interesting. This was the only one of the Ten Commandments that had a promise attached to it: honor your father and mother so your days will go well. But that promise could also be a caution: if you don't honor your father and mother, your days won't go well.

"I don't know about you guys," I said, "but sometimes I'm not very honoring to my parents. Especially after everything they've done for me. When was the last time any of us, myself included, publicly honored our parents for all they've done? If you're like most men, probably never. We're like the ten lepers Jesus healed. Only one came back to say thank you. So my challenge to you is that if your parents are alive, write each of them a letter of love and blessing. If they're deceased, write them a tribute letter."

"What's the point of writing to our parents if they've passed away?" asked one of the men.

"So that your children and grandchildren will know what they did to help shape you into the man you are."

I admitted to the men that writing a letter to my mom would be easy, but writing a tribute letter to my dad was a different story. When it came to Dad, I still harbored feelings of anger and disappointment. But God wanted me to forgive, and perhaps writing a tribute letter to my dad would be the first step.

I also realized that the "sins of the fathers" wasn't just theological mumbo jumbo; it had a very real application in the lives of a family over generations. It's what John Eldredge calls "the father wound" in his powerful book, *Wild at Heart*. Look at the statistic: 90 percent of the men in prison never knew their fathers.

That's sobering. So what's the solution? Blame our fathers for our problems? No. First of all, your father inherited his child-rearing skills from his father, who got his from his father, who got his from . . . you get the idea. If you're going to play the blame game, you're going to have to accuse everyone all the way back to Adam.

Hey, come to think of it, he's not a bad guy to blame!

But that wouldn't solve anything, would it? The bottom line is: we're big boys. We have choices. And if the sins of the fathers are ever going to end, they have to end with us.

After confessing to the men my struggle with writing a tribute letter to my dad, we all prayed and encouraged one another, then went our separate ways.

In the weeks that followed, we wrote and delivered our letters to our parents, and the response was beyond anything we could've imagined. Take my friend, David McCane.

"Lord, Make Me a Better Christian!"

David's a quiet man, an unusual trait for one of the top attorneys in Dallas. But there's nothing quiet about the way he expresses his passion and love for his family. The night before he was supposed to deliver his boxes to them, we all took a moment to pray over them. Here was David, seven boxes in front of him, leaning over those boxes with tears streaming down his cheeks and falling onto the boxes as he prayed for each person in his family. I remember his words well: "Lord, I wish I could be a better Christian. I wish I could be a better leader for my family. Please help me do that."

That next night, David presented his boxes and they were a huge hit, especially with his ninety-one-year-old mother, Dixie. As she opened her letter, David asked if he could read it to her publicly. She agreed and he proceeded to read his letter of love, blessing, and affirmation to the whole family. And as he did, the tears began to fall from his mom. When David finished, an amazing thing happened. All of the children and grandchildren stood one at a time in front of David's mom and declared words of love and affirmation, telling her how proud they were to have her as their grandmother and great-grandmother.

It was a night she will never forget.

Honor

Another man who experienced great joy during this time was Simon Crowther. Simon's from England and has a wonderful British accent. When he speaks, everyone listens—not only because of his accent, but also because of his incredible integrity and love for his family.

Simon was constantly teaching his three young boys about the Scriptures, and so he was thrilled to be giving each of his sons, his wife, and his mother a memory box. He decided to do this when his mother, who lived in England, happened to be in the States for a visit. He had the whole ceremony planned.

The minute she walked in the door, the kids brought her to the head of the table. Then Simon and his sons stood and honored his mother, reading to her a letter of blessing, love, and affirmation. When they were done, the kids applauded their grandmother for all that she meant to their father and to them. Needless to say, she was completely overwhelmed and moved.

Simon was so proud of how his boys handled themselves that he said to them later that night, "I want you to always remember what you did tonight. In honoring your grandmother, you honor yourselves. And honor is a critical part of being a godly man. I'm very proud of you."

His sons beamed. And there is no doubt in my mind that what Simon began that night will be repeated for generations in his family.

"I Am Blessed Because . . ."

Like the others, I also experienced great triumph. Although my dad had passed away, I decided to write my mom an "I am blessed because . . . " letter. It's the simplest way I know to bless someone. Simple but powerful.

Mother's Day was coming up, so I sat down at my desk and asked myself, "When it comes to Mom, what are some of the things I'm thankful for? Why am I blessed to have her as my mom?" I handwrote her a letter that took me ten minutes. The words just flew out of my pen! If you knew my mom, you'd understand why. She embodies the love of Christ. I've never known a more loving, kind, gentle, godly person. So coming up with things to say about her wasn't hard at all. The toughest part was figuring out what to leave out!

This is what I wrote:

"My dear mother, today I want to give you a blessing. I'm blessed to have you as my dear, caring mother. I'm blessed because you love the Lord Jesus. I'm blessed because you told me about my Savior. I'm blessed because you've been my prayer warrior. I'm blessed because you've modeled what real love is. I'm blessed because you've always given me wise counsel. I'm blessed because you've been my wonderful friend. I'm blessed because you've been such an influential grandmother. I'm blessed because you gave me a tender heart to love my children. I guess what I wanted to say today was . . . Mom, I'm blessed."

It took no effort to do this. I simply picked up my pen, wrote my letter, placed it in a beautiful frame, and then set a time with my mom to present it to her. That time just happened to be Mother's Day, but it doesn't have to be a special occasion. Believe me, when it comes to your mom, she'll consider any occasion you do this as special.

When Mother's Day came around, I read my letter to my mom in front of the whole family. She was so pleased and proud, she immediately hung it on her bedroom wall. It's there to this day.

And if you were to drop by my mom's house for a visit, the first place she would take you would be to see that letter.

chapter thirteen
⤞
A Letter of Tribute

Future generations of your family will never know you, so this is your chance to convey to them your family legacy.

*T*here's another reason why I am blessed. I'm blessed because my mom's alive so I can tell her how much she means to me.

But for some of us, our parents have passed away. Still, you can write them a letter of tribute. Some might consider this an exercise in futility, but as I told the men in my lunch group, such a letter carries with it great importance. Future generations of your family will never know you or the person of whom you write, so this is your chance to convey to them your family legacy. Remember Psalm 78:1-7? You can "teach [your] children, so the next generation would know them, even the children yet to be born." And what are you to teach them? "The praiseworthy deeds of the LORD, his power, and the wonders he has done." And why are you to do this? So your children's children "would put their trust in God and would not forget his deeds but would keep his commands."

Over the last few years, doing your family's genealogy has become increasingly popular and easy to do. With the advent of the Internet, it's amazing what information is available to you in an instant—both good and bad. The good part is you can research anyone or anything in a fraction of the time it used to take. Remember those days? If you're my age, you do. You'd go to the library, look through the card catalog, and find a book on what you were interested in. Then, if that book was there, you'd sit down and read through it trying to locate your information. But if the book wasn't at your local branch, you'd have to wait while it was returned, or while a copy was transferred from the main library. In those days, researching a simple topic could take weeks, even months. But with the Internet, today you simply sit down at your computer, type what you want into a search engine, and in a fraction of a second, you have millions of resources at your beck and call. I don't have a clue how it works, but the results are absolutely stunning!

So what does that have to do with the person who wants to write a letter of tribute? It means you can expand that letter into a genealogy of your whole family! You can start in the "old country," wherever that was, and follow your family to the "new world," tracing every Aunt Mary and Uncle Henry until you get to the person you're writing about. You can even talk about the events that surrounded their lives—recessions and depressions, inventions and scientific breakthroughs. Anything that influenced them. Consider it a time capsule, a glimpse into the past for future generations.

I had a good friend who did that very thing. She even went so far as to create a DVD that told the story of her family, complete with pictures. It was like a photo album containing pictures of family members, the town they lived in, headlines from newspapers, even pictures from major events—wars and deaths of presidents. Anything to give future generations a sense of the times in which they'd lived. It was quite extraordinary. PBS could take lessons from this lady.

I'm not suggesting everyone do this. It's a lot of work. And for a guy with seven kids, it could run as long as *War and Peace*. You'd have to put in an intermission. Not everyone has the time or expertise to take on such a task.

Realizing that, several years ago I created a company called Visual Biographies to help those who wanted something like this. Each biography is filled not only with pictures of the family but also of the times in which they lived. We even include home movies where appropriate. It's a wonderful way to capture the heart of a family.

Harder Than It Seems

The important thing is that no matter how it's done or what form it takes, you write your letter of tribute. That can be hard. Sometimes the memories you're left with aren't the kind you wish you had. Believe me, I know. I've already told you of my struggles with my dad. When I wrote my mom, the words just came flowing out. But when I sat down to write my letter to my dad . . . nothing. I can't tell you how many times I got up from that table and walked away, only to have guilt drag me back a few hours later. Of course I blamed all this on my dad.

"Look at what you're putting me through! If you'd been a better father, if you'd told me you loved me or showed me any affection at all, this would've been easy! But no, you didn't!"

Instead of a memory of love and affection, I was left with only emptiness. But if all that was my father's fault, then what kept drawing me back, full of guilt, to that table? Could it be God was trying to tell me something?

"Look, God, alright, I know it's probably partly my fault, but . . . "

There's always a "but." And because of that——though I'm not proud of this—I didn't get anything written. At first, guilt hovered around me, pestering me like a mosquito. But as time went by it got easier and easier to ignore. I kept telling myself I'd get back to it. Right after Thanksgiving. Then right after Christmas. Then it became my New Year's resolution.

But I didn't get it done.

I knew exactly what the problem was. My anger toward my father was clouding my vision of all the good things he'd done. Every time I tried to think of something positive, all the old anger and resentment would crowd their way in, pushing away all the good.

I knew the shame was mine. I knew the guilt was mine. I knew I was commanded by God to honor both my parents.

But I just couldn't do it.

I'll take love and care over eloquence and grammar any day.

*O*ne of the things I have always cherished about my mom is that she instilled in me an absolute confidence that there is a heaven. For those of us who know Christ, we are destined for that eternal home. This teaching has been a bedrock in my life. Since I first accepted Christ, I've always been cognizant of and preparing for eternity.

And so, long before starting the Letters From Dad group, on November 24, 1996, to be exact, I wrote the final letter of my life.

November 24, 1996

I was leading a Bible study in my home on the topic of heaven when I decided to put everyone through an exercise. Before passing out paper and pens, I instructed everyone in the group to go to separate corners of my house and write a letter that would express their love, affirmation, and anything else they might want to say to their family, as if this were the last conversation they'd ever have.

"What exactly should we say?" they asked.

"I don't know," I responded. "That's up to you. But I would suggest you fill your letter with the essentials of what you'd want to leave them, your final thoughts, and the important truths you'd want them to uphold after you're gone."

There was a somber mood in the room as we went to our separate areas, and it was accentuated by the fact that one of the men in the group had recently been diagnosed with cancer.

Sitting in my corner, I was shocked at how fast my letter came and how important it felt to me. After twenty minutes, I called the group back together to read what had been written.

The letter of the guy who had cancer was especially powerful, as if he saw the end of a road we couldn't yet see.

At the end of that evening, I put my letter in my Bible. It's still there. Hardly a week goes by that I don't take it out and re-read it.

My Last Letter

Dearest family,

I wanted to take this moment to share my heart with you, realizing that I'm not promised another day or moment on this earth. I wanted to remind you of some important truths, and to declare to you that our wonderful God has always been faithful to your father. He's promised the same faithfulness to you. He's the God that can be trusted. So when you're lost or confused, hurting or disappointed, sad or joyful, it doesn't really matter; this great God is always there for you. As your heavenly Father, He's the first to greet you each and every morning and the last one to tuck you in at night—no matter what your age. As you sleep, His tender eyes never leave you, and as you go about your day He smiles upon you. This awesome, great God has numbered your days, and He wants nothing more than to walk and talk with you each and every moment of your life. This all-powerful but incredibly personal God loves you so much. Never forget that He is the One who sent His only Son, Jesus, to die on a lowly cross filled with pain and shame. Why did He do that? So that you could spend forever in His presence. Always remember the price He paid for you.

I want to remind you of a few things: serve Him always. Read His Word daily. Talk to Him often throughout the day. Don't forget to tell others about this great gift of salvation. Love others because He first loved you. Serve others as He has served you. And please, please remember to tell my grandchildren and my great-grandchildren about this wonderful Savior. Tell them that though I've never met them, I pray for them. And as you enter heaven's gate, remember that I'll be there for you, applauding, cheering as you are welcomed by the Lord Jesus Christ to your eternal home. There, my dear family, we will live together as a heavenly family once more and forever.

I love you guys,
Dad

OK, it's not Shakespeare, and I have a pretty good idea what kind of grade I'd get in high school English. But do I care? Not a smidgen. I'll take love and care over eloquence and grammar any day. It's the final letter of my life, my final statement of what's important. Not someone else's. And though others might not think it eloquent, I know for a fact that Jesus grades on the curve.

"What's on the Mantel of Your Life?"

Remember Dave Dravecky, the famous baseball player who fought a bout with cancer? What an amazing story. He thought his baseball career was over, but sure enough his cancer went into remission and he began to train again. By the time baseball season began again, he was feeling pretty good, so he started pitching and winning some games. Then one night as he threw a particularly hard pitch, Dave's arm suddenly shattered. The whole stadium heard it explode. *Bam!* They said it was like a shotgun going off. Chuck Swindoll called it "the pitch heard around the world."

Obviously, the cancer had come back. Doctors ended up

amputating Dave's arm and shoulder. As everyone knows who's had cancer, a reoccurrence can be even scarier than getting cancer the first time. But fortunately, by God's grace, Dave's cancer was arrested once again, and Dave is still with us today. In fact, he's become one of the most powerful witnesses for Jesus Christ in the world of sports.

Let me ask you something. When Dave came face to face with death, what do you think mattered most to him? Do you think it was his mantel full of trophies? He's got a lot of them— some really impressive ones too. But none of that made a difference to him. So what did? Interestingly enough, what mattered to Dave was leaving behind a legacy—a letter.

"I'll never forget the day I gave my son a blessing," he says. "I sat down and wrote that letter, then I had the opportunity to read it in front of my son's third-grade class. It was one of the most precious moments of my life, one that I'll never forget. I think it allows our kids to see our heart. Through this act of love you are leaving a blessing that will impact your kids for eternity, and there's no better gift that any of us can leave behind for our children."

What's on the mantel of your life? Some of us have a lot of clutter up there, a lot of impressive but ultimately worthless accolades. We need to take that "stuff" off our mantels and replace it with what matters. Because when it comes time for you to write the final letter of your life, it's the things that really matter that you want to write about.

Dear Wanda,
I haven't
to write a
so I wi
must
me a
Ad
I
as
ge

S/Sgt Earl E. Vaughn
2nd Tech Sch Sq
Lowry Fld, Calif.

PLACE
ONE CENT
STAMP
HERE

CHICAGO
SEP 1

(PAT. OFF.)

T CARD

nda Nelson
dar, Texas
566

chapter fifteen
Our Final Meeting

Once death's door closes,
you've lost your last chance
to speak to those you love.

hen we met for the fifth and final meeting of our Letters From Dad lunch group, everyone was a little nervous. Why? We were there to write the final letter of our lives. How appropriate that our final meeting would be devoted to writing our final letter. As I began the meeting, I reminded the men that they should be keeping copies of their letters in their leather binders, including the final letter we were about to write.

"And make sure someone in your family knows it's in there," I reminded them, "so when you . . . you know . . . they'll know. Alright?"

Everyone nodded. They weren't looking at me or each other. And for a moment, no one spoke.

Ever been in a crowded movie theater during an on-screen love scene? It gets real quiet, doesn't it? The same thing happens when people start talking about death. Reverence, maybe? Fear? Probably both. As Christians we know death is just a beginning, but there's still that separation to deal with— the loss of those we love, even if only temporarily.

As the group sat there in silence, I couldn't help but think about all the friends who were no longer with us, all the funerals I had attended, and all the eulogies I had heard. So I broke the silence. "If our friends who've passed away had been able to speak at their own funerals, I wonder what they would've said. Have you ever thought about that? What would you say if you could speak at your own funeral?"

"I'd probably say a lot of I love you's," one of the men volunteered.

"And a lot of I'll miss you's," said another.

"And a lot of I'm sorry's," said still another, quietly.

Captain Schannep's Last Will and Testament

It's sad how many people die without getting the chance to say good-bye. Every year thousands of estates go into probate because the deceased failed to leave behind a will. None of those people thought they were going to die, just like most of us don't ever fully connect with the concept of our own death. "Death happens to the other guy, not to me." Sure, we all understand intellectually that it's going to happen, but emotionally? Naw, not us. And that's too bad. Because what that means is that we're losing our last chance to say something—anything—to those we love.

Once death's door closes, you've lost your last chance to speak to those you love. That is, unless you've discovered a way to speak from beyond the grave, like the father of my friend. No, we're not talking Houdini here. And we're not talking about some spiritualist mumbo jumbo. The Bible says once you're dead, you're dead. Finiti. End of story. And I agree, except in the case of Greg Schannep's father, who found a way to communicate with his son after his death— forty years after his death!

How did he do it? I'll let Greg tell you the story:

My name's Greg Schannep, and I'm a chaplain in the army. Some say you don't miss what you never had. Well, I never had a father, but I still missed him very much. Dad was a career Air Corp pilot who flew the famous Flying Fortress, the B-17. That's the plane he flew the day he was shot down somewhere between Japan and the Philippines during World War II.

I was four months old when my dad died, so I never knew

him. Without a father, I focused all my love on my mom. I was the fourth of four boys and probably grew up a little faster than I should have because of my father's not being around. Dad's death was hard on all of us, but especially hard on my mom. She never remarried and instead turned to drugs and alcohol to drown her pain. When I was fourteen, she died of a drug overdose. My life fell apart, and for the next ten years I did things I'm ashamed of. When I was twenty-four I heard the gospel. For the first time, I heard about someone who loved me and cared for me, and could make me a new person. It was awesome. I suddenly had a new life.

Six years later, I joined the army as a chaplain and served for ten years until one day, out of the blue, I received a phone call from my brother.

"Greg," he said, "I was going through some stuff in the attic the other day when I came across some old letters Dad had written Mom during World War II. You won't believe this, but as I looked through them, I found a letter addressed to you."

"To me?!?" I was astounded. "I don't understand.

"All I know," my brother said, "is that you need to come read this letter."

I can hardly describe how precious that letter was to me. He'd written it the day before his last mission, and in those pages, he said he just wanted to make sure that he wrote me to welcome me to the family. It was eight pages full of love and affirmation from a father I never met.

He was forty years old when he wrote it, sitting in a Quonset hut somewhere in the middle of a war, and I was forty years old when I read it—forty years later—sitting in the living room of his home.

It was as if those forty years just melted away and I could see my father sitting on his bunk—young, handsome, his life in front of him, taking the time to write his future son to give him his blessing.

That letter made my life complete. I received more love and acceptance from a father I'd never seen than most people get from fathers they see every day. That letter is my single most prized possession, and I will treasure it forever.

There's that word again. Treasure. Now, I'm not suggesting you take forty years to deliver your final letter to your children, but I think you can see the incredible power and responsibility such a letter carries.

MONEY IN A HURRY

TO

QU
ECONOM

chapter sixteen
Last Will and Testament

Go out like a lion, not a lamb.
Make a final statement.
Let people know you were here.

*W*riting the final letter of your life will be the hardest letter you'll ever write. After all, these are your parting words. What do you put in such a letter? What do you leave out?

That's why I told the guys in my lunch group, "As hard as this letter is to write, let me assure you, I'm going to pick on you until you do it. I care too much for you to not let you write this letter. I don't want to come to your funeral and have nothing from you."

Have you ever read Psalm 90:9? "We finish our years with a moan," it says. Well, that certainly wasn't going to be us.

"Go out like a lion, not a lamb," I challenged the men. "Make a final statement. Let people know you were here."

Slowly but surely the men began to write their letters. And slowly but surely they began to place them in their leather binders where they would remain until their death.

Their last will and testament.

"Pray That I Don't Die . . ."

Unfortunately, not all the men wrote their letters that day. My friend Jose Martinez was one of them. Remember him? He was the guy who ran an airline and was caught in multiple affairs before Christ made him a new man. Like the rest of the group, he was committed to writing his letter. But during our final meeting, he couldn't think of anything to write, so he told himself he'd just wait until he got home. When he got home there were phone calls to return and papers to read. When he awoke the next morning he thought, *I know I need to write my letter, so I'll do it at lunch for sure.* But then a lunch meeting popped up unexpectedly, and then there was another meeting, and then another. One day turned into a week and a week into a month, and pretty soon he'd forgotten about his letter. After all, he was a busy guy. There was a business to run, deals to be made, conferences to attend. He wanted to write his letter, but he just couldn't be bothered with it right now. Besides, there was plenty of time, right?

Wrong.

Two months later, Jose had a heart attack. It was bad. He technically died twice on the operating table. But by the grace of God, Jose pulled through. When I went to see him, he was still in bad shape, hooked up to every tube imaginable in the ICU. As I saw my friend lying there, I began to weep.

At that moment he stirred from the fog of anesthesia and looked up at me. I could tell he wanted to speak, so I leaned over, placing my ear next to his mouth. And what do you think he wanted to tell me? About some deal that needed to be handled or some important business call that needed to be made?

No.

"Pray that I don't die," he whispered, panic in his voice. "I haven't finished my letter."

Praise God, Jose didn't die. He got a second chance to write that letter. But we won't all get that chance. So don't wait. Do it now.

Trading Places

Years ago, I was wandering the northern English countryside when I came upon an ancient Saxon graveyard. I found myself staring down at one of the large slabs that marked a grave. Carved into the face of the tombstone in bold, intricate letters was the deceased's epitaph. It read,

> *I've often stood where you now stand,*
> *Looking down upon this mass of grass and sand.*
> *Oh, how I wish that in God's good graces,*
> *You and I could trade places.*

Now there's a guy after my own heart! He went out with a sense of humor. None of us want to die. But we will. Our only choice is how. Will we die at peace with man and God? Or will we die railing at death, our hearts filled with regret and disappointment?

I pray I will face my own passing as my mom faces hers: with grace and peace, surrounded by those she loves and who love her, and with eyes turned upward in expectation of a day when we'll all be together again in a place beyond pain.

I'll meet you there, Mom, and give you a hug.

Station hospital
May 28, 1943

Hello Darling
   I didn't d

Earl E. Vaugh
Feh Sch Sg
y Fld Colo,

Miss
2307.
Lu

Joe B brought me your
                    How that is
         u have ever
         s much like
              my hands off
            ok so cold
            Ha! Joe B

Will we leave those we love a legacy worthy of the time we spent here?

$\mathcal{A}$t this point, you may be saying to yourself, "All this blessing stuff sounds like a lot of hard work." And the truth is, it is. Like anything worthwhile, it will take commitment. But is it worth it?

Let me tell you a story about Princess Alice, the second daughter of Queen Victoria.

A Mother's Love

The year was 1878 and Black Diphtheria was sweeping through London, decimating the population. Princess Alice's youngest son was one of the hundreds of thousands who caught the disease. He was considered highly contagious, so the queen's doctors immediately took the young boy away from his mother and quarantined him.

"Stay away from him or you will surely die," they warned her.

She did as she was told but insisted on sitting outside her son's door day and night, despite the fact that it was the middle of winter. The only heat in the palace came from fireplaces, and there wasn't one anywhere near where the princess kept her vigil. At night, the cold corridors dropped below freezing. Though others begged her to move from the door, the princess refused.

Then one day she heard her son cry out in pain from the other side of the door. "Why doesn't my mother come kiss me anymore? Why doesn't she come visit me? Why doesn't she love me?"

It was as if an arrow pierced her heart, and the princess began pounding on the door, begging to be let in. The doctors refused, and so she pounded even harder, until her hands bled all over the rough wood.

The doctors pleaded with her to stop. "Please go away! We'll take care of your son! If we let you in, you will die!"

But she refused to leave and continued pounding until they finally agreed to crack the door open an inch so she could see her son. When they did, she forced her way in and ran to her son, smothering him with kisses and saying, "I'm here, my precious son, and I will never, ever leave you again."

A few days later, her son died.

And a few days after him, so did his mother.

They were buried together.

That's a mother's love. You may argue the child was selfish. You may argue his mother was foolish. But I dare say, if you were to ask her if it was worth it, I think we all know what the answer would be.

There are worse things in life than death.

We're all going to die. The only question that remains is will we die well? Will we leave this world a better place than we found it? And will we leave a legacy worthy of the time we spent here to those we love?

Teach Us to Number Our Days

During my final meeting with the men, I shared with them Psalm 90:12: "Teach us to number our days aright, that we may gain a heart of wisdom."

Counting your days and planning for the end of your life is wise. Many people make their own funeral arrangements in advance, hoping to save their loved ones the pain and hassle. But how many of us prepare our legacies? That would be wise as well. Take a look at the following chart:

LIFE EXPECTANCY TABLE—MALE

Your Age Now	Expected Years Remaining	Your Age Now	Expected Years Remaining
10	62.75	60	18.42
20	53.21	65	14.96
25	48.63	70	11.92
30	44.06	75	9.24
35	39.52	80	6.98
40	35.05	85	5.19
45	30.61	90	3.64
50	25.48	95	2.90
55	22.21	100	2.22

Source: HCFA State Medicaid Manual Part 3 - Eligibility § 3258.9.B (Table I)

According to this chart, the average American lifespan is basically 73 years. That's 26,561 days of life on average. Just for fun, let's figure out how much time you have left. Some of you may not think that sounds like a lot of fun (especially some of you older folks), but hang in there.

Looking at the chart, what do you see? Well, if you're thirty-five, you've still got thirty-nine Christmases ahead of you. Congratulations! But if you're seventy-five, you can skip the gift wrapping. You'd better get that final letter written!

Don't let someone else write your epitaph.

MEMPHIS
1951
FAIRGROUNDS AMUSEMENT PARK

BUY
DEFENSE SAVINGS
BONDS AND STAMPS

DENVER
NOV 11
1942
COLO.

God has already given me
my address in heaven.

*I*t's one thing to pass on letters of love and appreciation to your family; it's another to leave behind a legacy. So how can you enrich the heritage you have to offer others when you leave this earth? I've discovered four main ways.

1. Live Well—This is the most important thing. If you haven't done this, the other ways of leaving behind a legacy will be virtually pointless. Live your life in such a way that your family and friends will remember you well. It's that simple— and that hard. It doesn't mean you have to be perfect or that you won't make mistakes. It just means that every day you wake up and rededicate that day to becoming more like Christ, so that at the end of your life you can say as Paul did to Timothy, "I have fought the good fight, I have finished the race, I have kept the faith" (2 Timothy 4:7).

Note there are three parts to that declaration. First, Paul "fought the good fight." What had he been fighting for? To live a Christlike life and to tell others of the Savior. He did this in a "good" way, in a way that was honoring to the Lord. Secondly, Paul had "finished the race." He kept fighting to live a sanctified life and to spread the gospel all the way to his last breath. He didn't stop short of the finish line. He finished the race. And finally, Paul "kept the faith." He did as the Lord told him and never wavered. Others had fallen by the wayside, given in to the world's dangers and pleasures, but not Paul. He kept the faith.

My mom has done that. And I pray every day that I will do the same.

But what if you're clueless on what a life lived well looks like? How does it feel? Obviously, it's hard to live life this way if you don't know what it is in the first place. Fortunately, God gives His instructions for living well in Romans 12:9-18:

"Love must be sincere. Hate what is evil; cling to what is good. Be devoted to one another in brotherly love. Honor one another above yourselves. Never be lacking in zeal, but keep your spiritual fervor, serving the Lord. Be joyful in hope, patient in affliction, faithful in prayer. Share with God's people who are in need. Practice hospitality. Bless those who persecute you; bless and do not curse. Rejoice with those who rejoice; mourn with those who mourn. Live in harmony with one another. Do not be proud, but be willing to associate with people of low position. Do not be conceited. Do not repay anyone evil for evil. Be careful to do what is right in the eyes of everybody. If it is possible, as far as it depends on you, live at peace with everyone."

That's certainly enough to keep us busy! What a list. Thankfully, we can be assured that God would not have included all those things in His definition of a well-lived life if it weren't possible for us to follow through with them. With His Spirit guiding us, we can truly live a life worthy of a rich heritage.

2. Write Your Legacy—That's what this book is all about. As you've already learned, leaving behind a written legacy involves writing letters for the rest of your life, culminating in your final letter. This last letter is the most important of all your letters. It's your last chance to say the things on your heart.

If you're struggling to put those things in words, try this: Start with the phrase, "If you're reading this, I'm not here. And

so the most important thing I want you to know is
_____," then just fill in the blank.

3. Speak Out Your Legacy—Leaving behind an oral legacy is as old as recorded time. It's how our ancient forefathers passed down their stories to future generations. Have you ever read *The Epic of Gilgamesh*? It was the earliest recorded epic poem, written in the third millennium BC, more than a thousand years before Homer. Although it's a purely secular book, it speaks of the time between Abraham and Noah, and even mentions the Flood. But what's most amazing about this tale is that long before it was finally written down on clay tablets, it had been passed down from generation to generation by word of mouth. Thousands of years later, in this age of electronics, the best form of communication is still a conversation between two people. Not only can it have more impact that any other form, it's also the most memorable.

4. Visualize Your Legacy—Many people are videotaping their final letter. Why would they put so much time and effort into a simple letter? Because they understand its significance. It is their final statement to those they love, and it could potentially survive long after their death. They also realize that combining images with music can communicate emotion far better than any other means. The impact of a visual letter can often be unforgettable.

A Mother's Legacy

Recently when my mother was in poor health I felt God calling me to capture the heart of this great woman on film. I flew to her with a video camera and asked if she felt well enough to speak. She gave the thumbs up.

For the next three hours, I videotaped my mom talking about

her life before I finally got to the most important question of all: "If you could speak to your great-great-grandchildren, what would you say to them?"

I offered to let her think about it for a minute before I started taping, but she shook her head and said, "No, turn it on."

"There's a couple of things I want you to know about me," she said, speaking directly to the camera. "Whoever I am to you—your grandmother, your great-grandmother, whoever—I was not a person of power and prominence, but I was a person of prayer. And I have laid up for you in the throne room of God prayers that you will come to know the great God and Savior I have served for seventy-eight years. The next thing I want you to know is that God has already given me my address in heaven. So write it down. When you get there, come visit me real soon. I'll be living at the corner of Hallelujah and Praise Street."

Didn't I tell you my mom was a great lady? She would've understood Princess Alice—and done the same thing. Even as she nears the end of her life, Mom is still reaching out, not only to me but to all the future generations of Vaughns, encouraging us to live a life of honor and faithfulness to the Lord.

That's what your final letter should be all about: leaving behind a legacy of encouragement for the future. Even if you've made serious mistakes in the past, you have the opportunity to point future generations toward the ultimate hope for tomorrow, Jesus Christ.

chapter nineteen

A Turning Point

We'd written letters to our wives, children, parents, and the final letter of our lives.

*I*t was over. Letters From Dad, my lunch group, whatever you wanted to call it, was finally over. I'd brought fourteen of my best friends together to bless our families and we'd done it. We'd written letters to our wives, children, parents, and the final letter of our lives.

And now it was over.

If no one else was shocked, I certainly was. I couldn't believe how fast it had gone. All the men felt pretty good about themselves as they prepared to say good-bye for the last time. All except me. I hated to see it end. I'd had a good time. No, I'd had a great time. And I was going to miss these guys.

But it was time to move on. The Christmas holidays were coming and we were all looking forward to being with our families. For some of us, it would be a chance to share our latest round of letters. For all of us, it was time to be with our families, the people we'd set out to bless, to celebrate the greatest blessing of all, the birth of Jesus Christ.

A Christmas Miracle

It was during the Christmas holidays, however, that something amazing began to take place. It started with a phone call from the wife of one of the men in the group. She said she wanted to wish me a merry Christmas and to thank me.

"For what?" I asked.

"For giving me a new husband," she replied.

Well, I knew she was happily married, so obviously we weren't talking replacements here.

"He's not new," I replied. "He's still the same old guy. God's just unlocked his heart a little."

121

"Well, whatever happened, thank you. Our love has grown so much deeper."

I hung up, admittedly feeling a bit smug.

Well, hand me a bow and arrow, slap a diaper on me, and call me Cupid! Greg Vaughn, the love-meister!

But then the vision of me wearing nothing but a diaper popped into my head and my smug attitude quickly disappeared. (God does have a way of keeping us humble, doesn't He?)

A few hours later, my phone rang again. It was another wife wanting to thank me.

A few days later, my wife, Carolyn, and I bumped into another one of the Letters From Dad wives.

"Greg," she said, looking me straight in the eye, "I'm so grateful for what you've done for my family. Thank you."

What stories all these women had to tell! Stories of joy and excitement—and all because their husbands had learned how to bless their wives.

Boxes of Blessing

It wasn't just phone calls. After a meeting at my church one day I was walking down the hall when someone yelled, "Greg, wait!" I turned around and Dirk Howard's wife, Shannon, ran up and gave me a great big hug.

"I can't thank you enough!" she said.

"For what?" I asked.

"I've always wanted my Dirk to be a letter writer. My dad loved to write me letters when I was a little girl, and I've cherished those letters my entire life. And now to have Dirk doing the same, I can't tell you how that makes me feel! And then to see him turn around and give those beautiful, mahogany blessing boxes to our children . . . it's truly one of the most precious things that has ever happened to our marriage and our family. Oh, but I have to tell you a funny story. Our ten-year-old son is really into Nintendo, computers, the whole Electronic Age thing. So when Dirk gave him his box, the first thing my son said was, 'But, Dad, where do I plug it in?'"

"I've Been Kidnapped!"

Dr. Chris Stanford is a quiet man with a tender heart. A medical doctor. A man who spends every hour of every day helping others. Certainly not the kind of man one would suspect of being a kidnapper. But he is.

OK, so the person he kidnapped was his own wife, Michelle. And OK, so she liked it—no, actually she loved it. I guess even with kidnapping, it's the thought that counts. But the bottom line is, this quiet, tenderhearted man is a kidnapper! After all, Michelle said so, telling me the story, in all its gritty details, between the frozen food and produce aisles.

"As you know, Greg," she said, eyes still beaming with excitement after her ordeal, "Chris and I lead very busy lives. Between small children in the house and Chris's medical practice, we simply have had no time to ourselves. Well, Chris finally decided he'd had enough, so he decided to kidnap me! That's right, his own wife! He took off from work without telling me and paid for my mother to fly in. He picked her up at the airport, brought her to the house, and when she walked in the door, I couldn't have been more surprised.

"'What in the world are you doing here?' I asked.

"'I'm here to take care of your kids while your wonderful husband, my son-in-law, kidnaps you for the weekend!'

"With that, Chris whisked me off to a beautiful hotel where

we had a romantic dinner and he presented me with my box and letter—a letter of love that I never dreamed possible from my quiet, shy husband. That weekend was the most incredible weekend of my life, and I'll treasure it forever. In fact, I loved it so much, I spoke to three of my friends and they want their husbands to take your course!"

"My course?" I choked. "But I don't have a course."

"Well, you should," she said, handing me a slip of paper. "And here are their names. They can't wait to hear from you."

MONEY IN A HURRY

TO SEND IT

WESTERN UNION
TELEGRAM

Ever hear the still,
soft voice of the Lord?

$\mathcal{B}$rrriiinngg!!!

It was my phone ringing late one night.

"Hello?" I managed to mumble. I'd been dreaming of steak. I love steak, and my mouth still watered.

"Greg? Jan London here."

Jan and Dick London are friends from Santa Fe, New Mexico, where they own a hotel. I've known them for more than twenty-five years and their son, Richard, had been a part of my Letters From Dad group.

"Is there something wrong?" I asked, concerned.

"Yes, there is. I'm very upset with you."

"Me? What did I do?"

"I hear you're not having anymore of those lunches, and I wanted Dick to take your course."

"But I don't have a course. It was just a lunch. Well, actually several lunches, but . . . "

"I don't think you have any idea what you're doing," she said, interrupting.

It wasn't the first time I'd been accused of that, but this time I really didn't.

"Excuse me?" I stammered.

"If you don't continue this, you'll be depriving women all over the world of a blessing from their husbands. I believe Letters From Dad is the fulfillment of the prayers of millions of women who want to see their husband's hearts unlocked. Because only when their hearts are unlocked can they get in touch with their emotions and truly have a great marriage. Besides, Dick hasn't taken your course yet. So as soon as you get your next lunch set up, call me. No, better yet, call Dick."

A quick good-bye and she hung up. I lay back in bed. Carolyn mumbled something and rolled over. A car passed on the street outside, and light and shadow ran helter-skelter about my room like precocious children.

"Are you trying to tell me something, God?" I asked the ceiling.

The house breathed and creaked. Then . . .

Silence.

And so I drifted back to sleep with visions of filet mignon in my head.

It Isn't Avon Calling!

The next morning I was yet again jolted out of my sleep. Only this time it was the doorbell. I stumbled down the stairs, opened the front door, and there on my front stoop stood four lovely, rather sweaty ladies. One I recognized as Gail Dalton, whose husband had been part of our lunch group. The others I didn't know.

"Sorry to bother you," Gail said, smiling while catching her breath, "but I was just jogging by with my friends here, and I told them I'd gone to dinner with Randy and that he'd given me this beautiful box with a love letter inside . . . "

" . . . and I asked what the occasion was," interrupted one of the ladies.

" . . . and I said," continued Gail, "'No special occasion. It was just a gift to show me how much he loved me.'"

"Which none of us believed, of course," chirped one of the other ladies.

"Our husbands would never give us a gift unless it was our birthday," frowned another.

" . . . or they have a confession to make!" said another.

All four ladies giggled while I stood there looking confused, so Gail got to the point.

"Anyway," she said, swiping away a bead of sweat, "I told them about Randy's love letter and how amazing it was and how it was the greatest thing that's ever happened to me . . . "

" . . . so now we want our husbands to write us letters," twittered the one who liked to interrupt.

" . . . except our husbands couldn't write a love letter if their lives depended on it," said another.

" . . . so they're going to have to take your course," said the third.

"Well, I really don't have a course," I responded.

"Of course you do," said the interruptive woman, handing me a business card. "This is my husband's office number. Call him."

"I don't care what it costs," said another, handing me her husband's number.

"Me, either," said the third, handing me her husband's number. "And if he complains, tell him I'll sell his golf clubs."

With that, all three turned and jogged off leaving me standing on my porch.

"BUT I DON'T HAVE A COURSE!" I yelled after them.

No one was listening.

Hug Thy Neighbor

Gail's husband, Randy, had been one of the men I'd first invited to my lunch group. He had immediately agreed but asked if he could bring along his good friend, Mark Daniels. I said yes, of course, and both men really enjoyed their time together writing letters. In fact, they held each other accountable, making sure they each got their letters written.

Mark had done just like we planned—took his wife to dinner, then gave her the box after dessert. His handwriting looks like Egyptian hieroglyphics, so he typed the letter so she could read it.

"I hope you're not disappointed," he said as she opened her box. "It's not jewelry or anything."

Believe me, she wasn't disappointed. As soon as she started reading the letter, she started crying, so Mark had to read it to her. While he did, the whole restaurant seemed to be listening.

I guess they liked it, because when he was done, they applauded. His wife kept saying, "Wow!" over and over again. Then she told him, "I have never felt so loved in all my life. I knew you loved me . . . but I never truly felt it until now. Every woman dreams of being loved like this and having their man tell them. This is the most romantic thing you've ever done. And all I can say is . . . wow!!!"

On their way home that night, the couple passed Randy Dalton's house when Mark's wife suddenly yelled, "Stop the car!"

"What's wrong?" asked Mark.

"I have to thank Randy for getting you involved in that group!"

"But it's 9:30 at night," protested Mark.

"I don't care," she said. "I have to do this."

And so Mark stopped in front of Randy's house and waited in the car while his wife ran up to the door and rang the bell. When Randy opened the door, she threw her arms around him and gave him a big hug and said, "Randy Dalton, this has been one of the greatest nights of my life! No one has ever told me the things that Mark has told me and I have you to thank for that! So thank you! Thank you from the bottom of my heart!"

Randy protested. "Don't thank me; thank Greg Vaughn. It was his idea."

"But I Don't Have a Course!"

You can guess what happened next. The following day I got a call from Mark's wife telling me this story. She'd since told all her friends, and now her friends all wanted their husbands to take my course. "I really don't have a course!" I kept wanting to protest. But I didn't. Why? Because I suddenly heard a little voice inside my head whispering, "Well, maybe you should."

It was the voice I'd been waiting for that night, lying in my bed.

Ever hear the still, soft voice of the Lord? When I do, I've learned I need to listen.

So I started thinking. *OK, maybe I should . . .*

And that was a turning point.

When God opens a door,
a wise man steps through.

$\mathcal{N}$ot long after the holidays, two men from my original lunch group came to me and said they'd been involved in all sorts of men's movements, but nothing had ever touched them like Letters From Dad. They wanted me to know that if I decided to keep it going, they wanted to "march with me."

Wow. Amazing, huh? Problem was, I didn't know what I was called to do next. All I knew was that God had opened a door. And I knew from painful experiences in the past that when God opens a door, a wise man steps through.

So I brought together the original fourteen members of my lunch group. "Over the last couple of months, I've heard back from a lot of you guys and your wives," I said to them. "And everyone seems to think Letters From Dad really encouraged them."

They were all nodding. "It turned my marriage around," one guy said.

"Mine too," volunteered another.

"My kids loved their letters!" chimed in a third.

"So did my parents!" said still another. "The whole thing was a tremendous blessing to my family. And I really liked hanging out with you guys. Hated to see it end."

Everyone seemed to be in agreement.

"OK, so what does all that mean?" I asked.

"It means we should keep on going!" said one of the men.

"Lunch anyone?" laughed another.

And everyone began talking about where they wanted to eat.

"No, now wait a minute, guys! Let's stay focused here for a second," I begged. "I like lunch as much as the next guy, but if we're going to keep going, we'll have to do more than just eat, right?"

Everyone hesitated. They were thinking about it.

"So is this going to be like a Bible study, or should we try something else?"

"Like what?" asked one of the men.

And that's when I told the men I felt the Lord was calling me to do something different.

"You mean like teach a course?"

"No, not a course exactly . . . "

I was hedging, still fighting the idea of this being a "course." That smacked of something academic, and you know my experience with education. Besides, let's be honest here. I've never been to seminary. I barely graduated from college. About the only thing I was qualified to teach was how to balance a bowl of potato chips on your lap while watching the Super Bowl. Don't laugh. It's not that easy.

The truth is, people who teach courses have doctorates in something. And the closest I ever came to a doctorate was when a friend of mine let me hold his.

"So if it's not a course, what is it?" asked one of my friends.

The others looked at me expectantly. I had no idea.

"OK," said my friend, "then you're teaching a course."

And everyone agreed.

"Have you done anything like that before?" questioned one of the men.

I admitted I hadn't.

"What would you offer in this course?"

"I'm not sure. I guess everything we just learned about how to bless our families."

"To strangers?"

"Yeah, I guess so. Or maybe we could start with our friends."

"That's a good idea," said one of the men. "Kind of test the waters. Besides, it'll make my wife happy. Every woman in her Bible study wants her husband to take your course."

"How do you know?"

"'Cause she asked them. What do you say we have a dinner and invite all of them?"

And that's exactly what happened. These fourteen guys invited their buddies and anyone else who wanted to come to a dinner. And since they had a lot more friends than I did, 130 men showed up!

Legacy Groups

At this meeting, many of the original guys from my lunch group spoke about what Letters From Dad had done in their lives. Then each one turned to their buddies and said, "You need to go through this. It's a life-changing experience."

And sure enough, most of the men present committed to be involved.

Wow! This was a far cry from our first little lunch group of fourteen. That many men would require a much greater level of organization—not one of my strengths. Fortunately, some of the original fourteen were gifted in this. They suggested we break down the large group into smaller ones. That would encourage not only intimacy but accountability.

We decided to call these small groups Legacy Groups, and I asked the original team of guys to lead them. I gave each group two leaders, since that was how Jesus had sent out His disciples. In picking my Legacy leaders, I paired different personalities together—the gregarious, outgoing ones with the quiet, organized ones. That way the extroverts could be up front leading while the more detail-oriented ones could take care of the preparations.

The guys also suggested that at the start of each meeting, before they separated into their small groups, I should give an overview of what they'd be learning that night to the whole group. I was honored that they still wanted me to be the overall leader. So honored, in fact, that like a dummy, I volunteered to personally provide all the materials they would need: the right paper, boxes, pens, etc.

Big mistake . . . not because it was wrong for me to offer (after all, they'd have to pay me back) No, the blunder was letting me—or any guy, for that matter—go shopping.

chapter twenty-two
⌘
What Are You Up To, God?

Did I really want to do this?
Was this really God's will?
Will the Sox ever win the pennant?
Wait a minute!
The Sox did win the pennant!
Well then, anything's possible!

*a*s I traveled from meeting to meeting, speaking and delivering materials to all the men who were now attending the rapidly growing Letters From Dad group, I continued to wonder what God was up to. Where was all of this leading? Each time I asked, the same answer kept coming back: "Just keep going."

So I did.

Besides, things were really looking up. The new guys were experiencing the same joy our original lunch group had discovered. And the men from that original group were having a great time leading these new groups.

Me? I was having the time of my life! I would open each session with an overview, then watch like a proud father as the men separated into their small groups. I was also thoroughly enjoying preparing for my overviews, delving into Scripture as never before, each day bringing a new revelation on how to bless others. And in the process, I was actually developing what educators might call a curriculum, without even knowing what a curriculum really was. My course that wasn't a course was actually becoming, well, a course.

Even more encouraging was that the new guys were being so blessed by this course that wasn't a course that they were telling all their friends, who were telling all their friends, who were telling all their friends! Amazingly, after only a couple of months there were Legacy Groups all over Dallas. What seemed even more unbelievable was that these groups weren't meeting at churches or home Bible studies; all of them were meeting in the workplace—in business environments, usually right after work. That wasn't by design. It just seemed an office building was the easiest place for a bunch of businessmen to get together at the end of a busy day.

Two months into teaching my course that wasn't a course, I was starting to feel pretty good about all we'd accomplished. Tired, but good. And when I say tired, I do mean tired. Dummy that I was, I'd volunteered to supply all the materials for the groups—and now there were a lot of groups!

"What Am I Doing Here?"

Somewhere between purchasing 500 boxes, 500 packages of stationery, and 500 pens, seeing them delivered personally, then racing from group to group to give my little talk, I remembered thinking, *What am I doing here?!?* Maybe this wasn't such a good idea after all. I had a full-time job, and here I was using all my spare time to prepare talks, find and purchase tons of materials, and zip from meeting to meeting all over town.

To add to my stress, some of the new guys were asking, "I have some non-Christian friends who would be helped by this. Is it OK if I bring them?"

Once again I found myself saying, "Sure, that would be wonderful!" And I meant it. I just didn't know how I could keep this pace up.

Then one night, one of our new guys rededicated his life to Christ. He'd been a Christian for a while but had become spiritually bankrupt, allowing himself to fall deep into sin. Apparently, something clicked for him during our meetings, and his life was changed.

At that moment, everything suddenly stopped. I suddenly stopped.

That little voice was whispering in my ear again.

"That's what you're doing here."

Promise Keepers on Steroids

So the 14 beget 130, and the 130 beget 350, and the 350 beget 500. And the locations where we'd been holding our meetings were now too small, so our meetings had to be held over several different nights.

At one of these meetings, I bumped into an old friend of mine, Tom Dooley. Tom's a national Christian radio host and was one of the first men to help launch the group Promise Keepers. He was so impressed by what he saw that he asked if I would come on his radio program.

I could hardly believe it. Another door was opening. At this point I had so many doors opening I was starting to feel like Bob Barker. So I hesitated.

"Something wrong?" Tom asked.

"No, no . . . " I was doing that hedging thing again, buying time. Conflicting thoughts caromed about my brain like billiard balls.

Everything seemed to be moving too fast, and frankly it was beginning to frighten me. Did I really want to do this? Was this really God's will? Will the Sox ever win the pennant? Wait a minute! The Sox did win the pennant! Well then, anything's possible!

"So you'll be on the show?" Tom had no idea a war was raging inside my brain.

I was about to say something stupid like "I'll think about it" when I just happened to notice one of my original guys huddled in prayer with a man who had just accepted Christ. They both had tears in their eyes.

I turned to Tom and said, "I'd be honored."

Two weeks later I was on the radio. I'll never forget how Tom began our interview. "Folks," he said, speaking into the microphone, "I'm gonna tell ya about the next great men's movement that I believe is about to happen in our nation. It's called Letters From Dad, and the only way I know how to describe this is it's Promise Keepers on steroids."

chapter twenty-three
⤖
The M Word

The silence was deafening.
And then I couldn't wait any longer.

*T*he cat was out of the bag. Suddenly I was receiving phone calls and e-mails from men who wanted to participate in Letters From Dad—men like Robert Blankenship.

"Hi, my name is Robert Blankenship. I just heard you on that radio show and almost had a wreck pulling off the freeway to write down your phone number!"

I could hear the sound of cars racing past in the background. "You'll have to forgive me," he continued breathlessly. "I'm a little frazzled."

I asked if he'd like to call back when he got somewhere safer.

"No, no, I'm fine now and I've got to ask you a question. I'm a single father. My wife left me and we just went through a terrible divorce that's left me heartbroken. And not just me. My twenty-year-old daughter's taking this really hard. And I was just wondering if there was anything in Letters From Dad that might help her."

I told him there was and asked if he would like to have lunch. He seemed genuinely thrilled.

The next day at lunch, I shared with him what we were trying to accomplish in Letters From Dad. He shuddered at the idea of writing a letter of blessing to the wife who had just divorced him, but he perked up when it came to sending one to his daughter.

The next week Robert showed up eager to learn. He was a banker, an analytical person by nature, with a heart of gold. But having a systematic approach to things meant he had to have

147

everything progress step-by-step. And as I talked him through the journey of letter writing, he took copious notes and asked tons of questions. When it finally came time for him to write his daughter's letter, he agonized over it for weeks, writing and rewriting until I thought he was going to have a nervous breakdown.

The night before he presented his letter to his daughter, he asked if he could read it to the group. We readily agreed.

He stood up, letter trembling in his hands, and said, "Guys, I'm really nervous."

"Don't worry," I reassured him. "We're all friends here."

"No, you don't understand. I'm not worried about you guys. I'm scared because I don't know how my daughter's going to respond. I've never said these things to her before."

I again encouraged him, and he began to read. It was beautiful, straight from the heart. After he finished, we assured him it was going to be a real success, and he committed to deliver it to her the next night.

Recalling his nervousness, I said a quick prayer for him that night.

I shouldn't have worried.

The next meeting Robert came waltzing in with his face beaming.

"Well, I did it," he grinned proudly. "Or I should say, God did it! Went to dinner with my daughter and it couldn't have gone better! I had her box engraved with her name and gift-wrapped, and when I gave it to her, she was so surprised. She kept talking about how beautiful that box was, and then when she read my letter she was overwhelmed with emotion. It was the most wonderful time I've ever spent with my daughter. She heard my heart and I heard hers, and our relationship now is stronger than ever. Thank you. Thank you so very much!"

Robert was so excited that he told his pastor about Letters From Dad, who then called to see if I would have breakfast with him. When we met, he told me he'd never seen such a change in a man as he'd seen in Robert, and he was so impressed he wanted to make the "course" an integral part of their entire men's ministry.

Letters From Dad had become an M word.

A ministry.

One Small Step

A ministry?!? Even now as I type that word, I shake my head in disbelief. How could I have a ministry? I was just getting used to this being a course. Preachers have ministries, not guys like me. Sure, every Christian is supposed to be "in the ministry," right? But there's a difference. I'm not a trained theologian.

I began reasoning with God. "OK, Lord. I don't know where You're going with this, but You opened the door and I stepped through. And since I know steps are best taken one at a time, I'm just going to take the next little step and trust You for the result, OK?"

Silence.

"OK, Lord?"

More silence. Was God ignoring me? Had I done something wrong? If He didn't want me to start a ministry, He could just tell me, right? I wouldn't mind.

Well, maybe I would just a little. Actually, a lot. I mean, I really felt like He was calling me to do this. So what was the deal? Why wasn't He talking to me? Didn't He know I was facing an important decision here?

"Alright, here I go, Lord. I'm taking that step. See me

stepping? This is me stepping here, Lord. Got my foot in the air . . . ready to take that next big step."

Even more silence.

I was getting desperate.

"One small step for man, one giant leap for mankind!"

Still silence.

My foot hovered in the air. I stood at a crossroads. Things were happening too fast—doors opening left and right—and I'd been stepping through them like I knew what I was doing. But I didn't.

Did I really want to take this to the church? Did I really want to make this a ministry? Did I really want to drop everything and commit my whole life to this? I really didn't know.

"Lord, I've got some big questions here that need answering. So if I don't hear from You, I'm just going to assume You want me stop, OK?"

Nothing.

"Lord, are You there?"

The silence was deafening. And then I couldn't wait any longer.

So I stopped.

November 10, 1942.

... to believe that
... service or
... when you wrote
... to Lubbock ...
... address because
... letters and
... you didn't
... had just about
... had took
... Lubbock has
been the starting place for a lot of
the kids and it has been so long
since I saw you, well, you know
what I mean! Yesterday your second
letter came and I had planned
to write last nite but Paul came
over about 2 O'clock and wouldn't let
me finish anything that I started.
Last nite Joe B. Nelson, Paul and
myself went to ... "... Inn
Inn" but there ...

*"God can't use you greatly until
He breaks you mightily."*
– Chuck Swindoll

*A*fter the spring session of Letters From Dad, I told the men I needed to take the summer off to try and get some direction from the Lord. The truth was, I was just plain scared and I had some doubts and fears that needed to be addressed.

Doubt is a terrible thing. I've often wondered about the disciples. Here these guys were, hanging out with the Lord all day, watching Him perform miracles and saying all this cool stuff. I mean, if anybody should've lived a doubt-free life, it was those guys! But until Jesus appeared to them after His resurrection, some of them still questioned if He was really everything He said He was.

Now don't misunderstand me. I've never doubted if Jesus is Lord. I'm absolutely convinced He is. But when it comes to knowing the right thing to do, sometimes I struggle. Not with the things instructed in the Bible but what isn't in the Bible. Those everyday decisions, like what you're supposed to do with the rest of your life.

We all know the pat answer: "Just follow the Lord's will." But how do you know what that is? How do you know what to do if God doesn't tell you? What do you do when the Lord quits whispering in your ear?

Moses Was a Wimp

At least that's what I used to think. And I'm not talking about when he led his people out of bondage. I'm talking about before that, when he was complaining to God, "O Lord, I have never been eloquent, neither in the past nor since you have spoken to your servant. I am slow of speech and tongue" (Exodus 4:10).

Can you believe that? God Himself spoke to Moses, telling him exactly what to do . . . and what did Moses do? He argued with Him. I never could understand that. That is, until I found myself in a similar situation.

Obviously, I didn't have the children of Israel to lead out of slavery. No rivers to part. No miracles to perform. Just a few hundred guys who depended on me to know what I was doing.

And I didn't.

Damaged Goods

One night as I was struggling with all this, I stood in my backyard staring up at heaven, trying to imagine myself from God's perspective—like a minuscule speck in a satellite photo. At least that's how I thought God saw me. Totally inadequate. The wrong guy for a ministry.

After all, I was just a poor kid from Lubbock, Texas. I'd never been to seminary. I wasn't a public speaker or a writer. I was even dyslexic, for goodness sake! (I know you know all this, but I was beginning to wonder if God did!)

"I know why You're not talking to me, Lord," I told Him. "You know I can't do this and You're trying to let me down easy. Believe me, I understand. I can't do this. I admit it. I'm the last person to be teaching others about how to bless their families. Absolutely the very last person!"

Why was I so sure of this? Simple. My history proved it.

Because at one point in my life, I was almost ruined by the breakup of my own family. Like most people, I had always painted a picture of my life that included a wonderful, loving marriage, three or four kids, and a two-story house with those happy kids hanging out of every window. (Not literally, of course, but you get the idea.) There was even a time when I had all that. Until one terrible day when my idyllic world came crashing down.

Chuck Swindoll has a great quote that says, "God can't use you greatly until He breaks you mightily."

And that's exactly what God did to me. Before my divorce, I'd often heard Chuck use that quote, but it never came home to me until after sixteen years of marriage and four wonderful children, my life came apart. In the midst of all that pain, I kept asking God, "Why? How could You let this happen? It not only violates Your Word, it violates everything I've ever dreamed of and hoped for and believed in. So tell me, Lord," I begged, "how could You have let this happen?"

And God said . . .

Silence.

chapter twenty-five

The Brady Bunch . . . Plus One

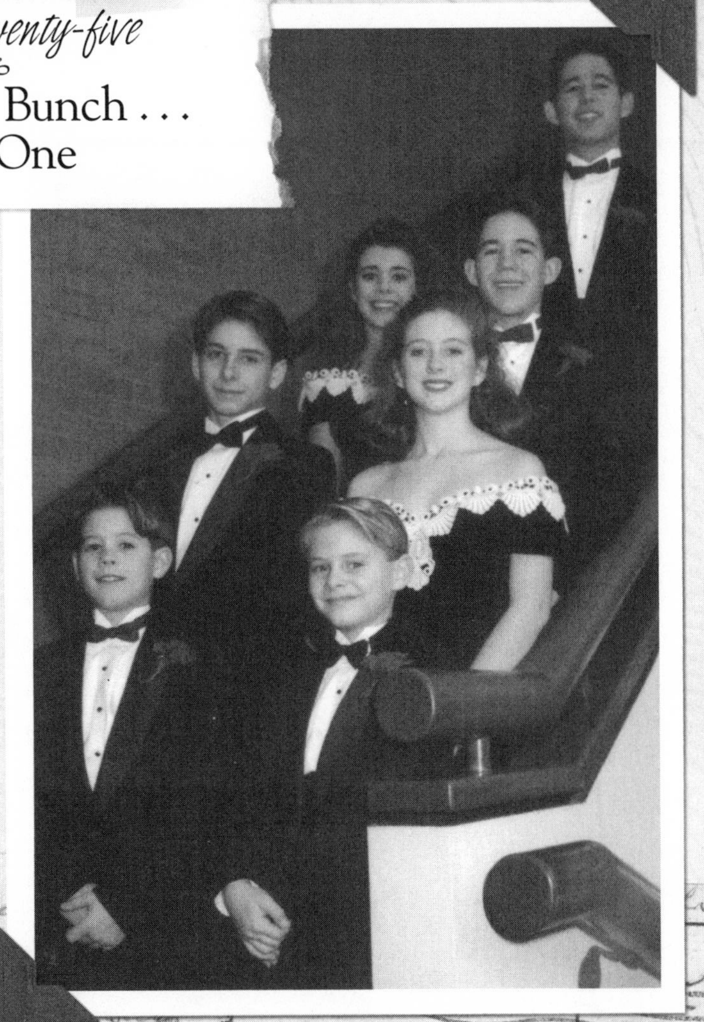

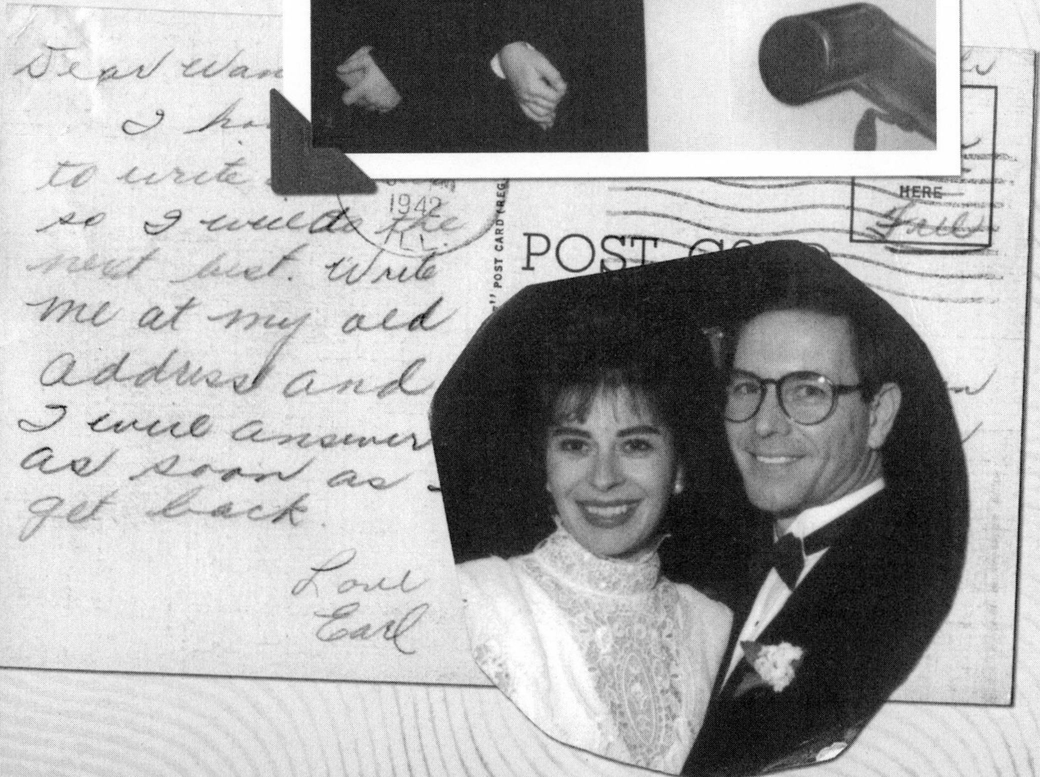

There I was, the guy who was never,
ever going to marry again . . .

The only thing that kept me together during my divorce was my desire to be a great father to my kids. I still wanted to be a living example of Christ to them. But that seemed hard when my kids were firsthand witnesses of the destruction of their parents' marriage.

After I'd been divorced for three years, I finally decided it might be good for me to fellowship with other Christians who'd been through a similar experience. I thought about attending a class for divorcees at my church, Fellowship Bible Church North, in Plano, Texas.

Before I did, I called the leader of the group and asked if we could meet. Over lunch the next day, I told him I was interested in attending his class but informed him that dating again wasn't an option for me, and I certainly wasn't looking for a mate in his class.

He smiled and nodded. He'd heard that before.

Yeah, but I meant it.

The next week, I walked into the class feeling nervous and a bit reluctant. Was this something I really needed, or was this a pseudo-dating service disguised as a church group? The more I sat there, the more I wanted to bolt. But as the meeting progressed and we went around the room introducing ourselves, my eyes were suddenly riveted on this beautiful lady sitting across from me.

Talk about psychobabble running rampant in my mind! On the outside I sat there with this half-crazed smile on my face, but inside I was screaming, *What in the world are you doing? Why are you staring at her?*

I couldn't help myself. So after the meeting was over, I went over to her and said, "Hi, my name is Greg and I have four wonderful kids."

And she said, "Hi, my name is Carolyn and I have three wonderful children."

What did she just say? She has three kids? Let me see now . . . my four plus her three equals . . . seven kids! I may be lousy in math, but no matter how you added it up, seven kids is a bunch! Was I out of my mind?!?

Wait a minute, I am out of my mind! Why am I worried about seven kids? It's not like I'm going to marry this lady! I'm never, ever going to marry anyone ever again, remember?

And the next week, just to make sure everyone understood that I was never, ever going to marry anyone ever again, I went to see my good friend and pastor, Dr. Gene Getz and told him so.

"What brought this up?" he asked, smiling.

I told him I'd met Carolyn Rogers.

"Ah," he said, "Why didn't I think of that?"

Little did I know that after Carolyn's divorce, Gene had been watching over her, protecting and caring for her.

"She's a wonderful woman," he said.

What did I care? She could've been the finest woman who ever lived; I still wouldn't have been the least bit interested. I was never, ever going to marry anyone ever again.

Ever.

Gene was still smiling across his desk. "Maybe you two should go out."

Wasn't anyone listening to me? Had I not just said I was never, ever going to go out with anyone ever again? Or was it marry? I was getting confused. Either way, I was sure of one thing. In order to marry someone you have to go out with them first, right? So since I vowed to never marry anyone, I was going to cover my tracks on the dating game as well. I had a new addition to the rules: I would never, ever go out with anyone ever again!

No one could talk me out of it. I'd made my decision. And it was final.

One week later, Carolyn and I began dating.

Family Style

It wasn't your usual dating arrangement. We dated as a family. Between the two of us, we had seven kids under the age of eighteen, and they all went along on our dates. It was like having your own youth group. Fortunately, our children fell in love with each other.

They weren't the only ones. Gene had been right. Carolyn was a wonderful woman. She was a Ruth and Rachel and Mary all rolled into one, with a little bit of Sarah thrown in for good measure. But Gene had forgotten to mention one other thing. Not only was Carolyn beautiful, smart, and kind, she had the voice of an angel. When I sang, dogs came running. When Carolyn sang, the heavens parted.

Of course there was still the problem of all those kids. What would they think of our marrying? I'd told Carolyn from the beginning that I would never remarry unless I had the absolute blessing of all my children—and hers.

One holdout, no marriage.

It turned out to be a nonissue. One day my kids approached me with a request. "Dad, all of us kids have talked about it, both Carolyn's kids and us, and we want to be a family. And since you're not getting any younger . . . " Kids say the darndest things, don't they? " . . . and since you're never, ever gonna find anyone better than Carolyn," they continued, "why don't we get this thing going?"

A few months later, with a church full of smiling people, we all stood at the altar—the whole family. There I was, the guy who was never, ever going to marry again, exchanging vows with the most beautiful songbird who ever lived. Solomon would've been jealous.

When we were done, Gene led all seven of our kids in a vow of commitment to the Lord, to each other, and to us as their parents. Then he turned to Carolyn and me and said those magic words, "I now pronounce you man and wife!" And as the nine of us traipsed up the aisle past friends and family, the church organist piped out the music from *The Brady Bunch*.

It was true; we were the Brady Bunch—plus one. Seemingly overnight, I found myself with a wife and seven kids all living under the same roof. We had so many cars out front it looked like the parking lot at Wal-Mart.

But I didn't complain. God was so good. He had healed the pain of my divorce and used that brokenness to give me a tender and compassionate heart toward the men who were now going through Letters From Dad. More than 40 percent of the guys in our Legacy Groups were divorced. It wasn't by chance that the complex issues I had faced helped me find common ground with these men. It was God's sovereignty.

A Completed Heart

So as I stood out by my pool that night, protesting to God that I was inadequate, I suddenly realized something.

God was never silent. We just don't listen sometimes.

In that moment, my mind cleared as a cloud clears from the moon, and God spoke. "I've stood by you through everything. Do you honestly think I would desert you now?"

And that's when a Bible verse came to mind. "For the eyes of the LORD range throughout the earth to strengthen those whose hearts are fully committed to him" (2 Chronicles 16:9).

"OK, Lord," I said. "I'm not adequate, but if You can use me, I'm here."

And He answered: "You're right. You're not adequate . . . but I am."

Scenes in Cedar Breaks, Southern Utah. This is one of the many marvelous formations in this district, and a trip through Cedar Breaks by those visiting Bryce and Zion's Canyon should not be omitted.

THIS SPACE FOR MESSAGE

Will write when get to Salt Lake.

Earl

Published by Carpenter Paper Co., Salt Lake City, Utah

ADDRESS

Miss Wanda Nelson,
Matador, Texas
Box #566.

chapter twenty-six

The Lost Art of
Letter Writing

*There's no such thing as a
bad letter that ends with
the words "I love you."*

That fall, I jumped back into Letters From Dad with an overwhelming sense of God's blessing and purpose, determined to build a ministry worthy of that trust. We were no longer just a bunch of friends getting together. We were a ministry. With God's guidance, we could potentially touch the lives of men all over the world.

One of the problems we faced, however, was that the vast majority of men attending our seminars wouldn't be professional writers. That certainly included me. Although those first letters I wrote to my wife and kids were heartfelt, I certainly could've benefited from a little professional advice. So I asked a good friend of mine, Dr. Reg Grant, who is the director of media arts in ministry at Dallas Theological Seminary, to help me develop a writing curriculum for the men. Reg has been teaching creative writing for more than twenty years at the seminary and has been writing to his own children even longer. When I asked if he might provide our men with a few pointers, he graciously agreed.

So how can you craft letters that truly express what's in your heart and soul? Here's some advice from Reg.

"Write—Just Do It!"

When you first begin a letter, the title above says it all. "Write—just do it!" Don't let that blank page or screen intimidate you. Just start writing. It's not as important that you write in full, complete sentences that would garner you an A in English as it is that you get something—anything—down onto the page. Don't judge yourself. Whatever you put on the page can be rewritten. It's not cast in stone. You're not coming down from Sinai with two smoking tablets in your hand. You're putting words on paper that can be crumpled up and thrown away. (Well, obviously not if you're using a computer . . . but you get my point.) The key here is, don't just stare at a blank page; get some words on the paper. Any words.

Here are a few ideas to help you jump-start a great letter. These will at least give you a broad understanding of how to write. When beginning a new letter, the first question I always ask myself is, "Why am I writing? What is my purpose?" Your purpose might be to tell your daughter how much you love her. It may be to apologize to your wife for not spending enough time with her lately. Whatever it is, make it specific. You may want to write out your purpose on another sheet of paper so you can refer back to it.

Start at the Beginning

Your first sentence is the most important. You want to hook your reader. What kind of first line might you come up with? It's your call. You might start with something fun, like a joke, for example. Or you might want to begin with a shared memory, something that will grab them because they experienced the event themselves.

Here are four ways you can begin a letter:

1. With a story—I began one of my favorite letters that I ever wrote this way: "Mom stood on the icy road and watched helplessly as Dad's car slid down the mountain toward the guard rail." A true story. It engages the reader so that they want to find out if Dad's car went over the edge or if Mom was able to rescue Dad.

2. With a great quote or a startling statement—Something that makes the reader go, "Aha!" For example, "If I were a

betting man, I'd wager that heaven tastes like chocolate." It's unusual enough to catch your attention so you will read on.

3. With a summary of what will be discussed—For example, "This summer I'm planning on pulling a Steinbeck. I'm going to drive all the way across the country, reminiscent of John Steinbeck's book, *Travels with Charlie*." This is a summary, or overview, of what you'll be talking about.

4. With a "Hey you!" line—A "Hey you!" line is personal. It makes direct reference to the reader using something that is shared. Some of the most effective letters you'll ever write will deal with those memories that you have in common with your family. Whenever you use something that's precious to both of you, you automatically draw the reader into that relationship. "I remember the first time my eyes met yours . . . it was like magic."

How to Tell a Story

As you begin to write your letter, stories and ideas may just flow out of you. The problem is that sometimes these stories and ideas are unrelated to each other. Your stories may have taken place over a lifetime and involve different people your reader has never met. And while you may have tons of ideas, the hard part is organizing them. So how do you weave all these divergent stories and ideas together? By striving for what I call unity. A letter that focuses on one idea is more forceful, more potent, than a letter that contains five, six, or seven random ideas in it. Stick with one simple idea.

You achieve unity through:

1. Subject—For example, the subject of one of your letters might be how you became a Christian. By keeping the focus on your testimony, everything you write about will revolve around

that one simple idea. That's unity through subject.

2. Incident—Focus on an incident or event that was poignant, tragic, disappointing, or exciting in your world. For example, your kids would probably love to hear about the day they were born. What was going on in the news that day? How did you and your wife respond to their birth? That's unity through incident.

3. Theme—What do I mean by unity through theme? Let's draw an example of theme from a well-known passage from Scripture. In Ephesians 6:10-20, Paul says that a believer needs to put on the armor of God. He goes on to describe each piece of that armor. So what's his theme? How to put on spiritual armor. That's unity through theme.

4. Point of View—One of the first things to do when you start writing is to decide whose story you're telling. Are you telling your story? Then make it your point of view. Even if you're describing something that happened to someone else, you can still tell the story from your point of view, as if you're seeing that person's story through your eyes. That's unity through point of view.

Wrapping It Up

How should you end your letter? That can be difficult. Obviously, you don't want to be like a plane hovering over the field until it runs out of gas and crashes. You want to land safely and smoothly so people will want to read your next letter. Often the best way to do that is to close with a carefully selected Bible verse. Find a verse that fits what you've been talking about and bring that verse to bear. Show how it applies to the life of your reader.

Another suggestion is to conclude with a statement of hope

for the future. Avoid ending on a down note; instead, leave the reading looking ahead with expectation.

Writing Is Rewriting

Once you have something down on paper, the real work (and the real joy of writing) has just begun. Writing is rewriting. Never expect to get it right the first time. You'll want to go back over what you've written and make it clearer and better. When you first start your letter, the goal is to simply get some words down on paper. But as you rewrite, the emphasis changes to getting the right words down on paper.

Mark Twain said it well: "The difference between the almost right word and the right word is the difference between the lightning bug and lightning."

However, let me caution you not to try and impress your reader with your big vocabulary. Simply write to communicate. Use words that will dramatically convey the idea you want to express. Usually, the more honest and to-the-point you are, the better.

You can also include dialogue. It's one of the best ways to achieve poignancy. Hearing, or in this case, reading what people have said lets you get inside the speaker's head. It helps the reader know what the speaker was thinking. "Give me my book right now!" is much more powerful than, "He told the man to hand over his book." Let the reader eavesdrop on the conversation. "This is what I said, this is what she said, this is what he said . . . " and so on, until your reader can virtually hear the conversation in his mind. And don't worry if the dialogue isn't grammatically correct. Put it down just the way it happened. The memory will be fresher, more realistic, and you'll have more fun writing it.

Also remember to skip an extra space before starting each paragraph. Your letters will seem easier and faster to read if there's an extra bit of white space between paragraphs, and your lines won't seem so jumbled together. And last, but certainly not least, if you're writing on a computer, be sure to use your word processor's automatic grammar and spell-check. You'll be amazed how many mistakes it can catch.

When you boil it down, writing a letter isn't so hard. It's usually not a matter of what you want to say; it's finding how to say it. Remember, the best way to start writing is to simply write. Get words down on paper. Then take the time to rewrite, making sure you have the right words. As you write, strive to make your writing visual, since most of us best retain those things that are visual. Then finally, edit your letter so that you wind up communicating exactly, precisely, creatively, accurately, clearly, what God has given you to say. And never forget, there's no such thing as a bad letter that ends with the words "I love you."

It was as if God were saying to all of us, "What I have joined together let no man, or woman, put asunder."

*S*tarting a new ministry can be pretty intimidating. And so as we began, I was like a sponge, soaking up any helpful information I could find. Reg's assistance in developing a writing curriculum was invaluable, but I still had a lot of basic questions on how to build a ministry.

About this time, I heard about a men's conference featuring Dr. Ken Canfield that was being presented by The National Center for Fathering. Thinking I might be able to pick up some pointers, I went to the conference and had the opportunity to meet with Dr. Canfield. When I shared with him what I was doing, he was extremely helpful and supportive. He even suggested I place some materials I'd brought with me on a table in the foyer.

Then just before our lunch break, Ken got up in front of the whole conference and announced, "Gentlemen, I believe the eyes of the country should be focused on a new, emerging ministry called Letters From Dad. There's a table in the foyer and you need to pick up some material." I was flabbergasted. And to my astonishment, hundreds and hundreds of men overwhelmed our little table, taking everything in sight.

Boy, did that jump-start things! At the next Letters From Dad dinner, 600 men showed up. The phones began ringing off the hook with calls from all over the country as men who had attended our group started telling others.

Another Christmas Miracle

One of the men who began attending Letters From Dad at this time was a man named Richard. When I first met him, he was happy, cheerful, and eager to begin his letter-writing journey.

He shared with me how he had adopted his new wife's two children, and that he planned on giving his wife and kids their letters of blessing for Christmas. He couldn't wait to learn how to do that.

But the first week in December, Richard suddenly quit coming. I didn't see him again until after the holidays when he showed up at our January meeting. He looked like a different man. Gone was the happy-go-lucky smile and the cheerful excitement. In their place was the somber countenance of a man who'd been through a battle. When I asked him what was wrong, he began to share his story in front of the whole group.

"I love to read my Bible before going to work in the mornings, and that's what I was doing early one Monday morning the first week in December when my wife came in and asked if she could speak with me.

"'Sure!' I said, expecting a discussion of one of the children's schedules.

"We'd been experiencing some problems in our marriage, but I never would've imagined the next words I heard.

"'I want a divorce,' she said. 'And please don't argue with me or try to change my mind. I just want you to leave the house and get an apartment ASAP.'

"Still in shock, I went apartment hunting that afternoon after work. I found one and was about to put down a deposit when I felt the Lord say to me, 'What are you doing? Your wife told you to leave, but I didn't.'

"'Is there a problem?' the manager asked as I stood there with checkbook in hand and a blank look on my face.

"'Um, yes,' I replied. 'I . . . uh . . . I'm terribly sorry, but I'm afraid I don't need the apartment after all.'

"And with that I walked out and drove home. When I told my wife what the Lord had said, she wasn't a happy camper. But that didn't matter. God had told me to stay, and I was going to stay.

"An uneasy truce hung over our house all the way to Christmas morning, when I went ahead and presented her with her Memory Box and letter. She read the letter, nodded, mumbled something, and that was it. For some reason, she agreed to go to church with me that night, and what did our pastor end up speaking about? The fact that we all wear masks sometimes to hide behind—masks of insecurity and fear. He also talked about how we dishonor our mates by speaking words that hurt them.

"I could see the spirit of God working in her heart and she suddenly began to weep. And then to the shock of everyone, myself included, she actually stood up in the middle of the pastor's sermon and told everyone what she had done. She told them how I had obeyed God and refused to leave, and how angry that had made her at the time. But now she was thankful I had refused to give up on their marriage. She then asked for my forgiveness."

Miracles in Our Midst

By the time Richard had finished his story, you could hear a pin drop in the room. Many of the men there were divorced, and a few of them were going through a divorce at that very moment. It was as if God were saying to all of us, "What I have joined together let no man, or woman, put asunder" (Mark 10:9; paraphrased). What followed was an amazing and powerful time of those men surrounding Richard and giving him words of encouragement—some in the midst of their own trials.

Christmas is a time for miracles. It's when God sent His Son to be born in a stable as a sacrifice for our sins. The world has never seen a greater miracle than that. You may think that was the last miracle, that God's done with His miracle-working. I beg to differ. And there could be no finer proof than for you to come to Dallas and let me introduce you to Richard.

He will gladly tell you about the time God melted a frozen heart.

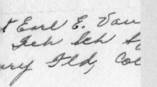

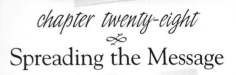

*We could never have imagined
the truly amazing thing
that happened next.*

*R*emember Robert Blankenship, the man who almost wrecked his car when he heard me on the radio? Well, one of the other miracles that happened during this time is that we started working with the men's ministry at his church.

Robert attends Parkway Hills Baptist Church, and his pastor, Pastor Dennis, has kept journals for decades. He even loves to write special messages to the people in his congregation. Pastor Dennis immediately saw how Letters From Dad could touch the hearts of his men.

"Look what it's done for Robert!" he said. "Now all we have to do is get every man in our congregation involved in the group," he told me, beaming with enthusiasm. "Then we'll use those men to reach out to the community. To kick things off, would you be willing to speak at a men's conference we have coming up at the church?"

"Sure," I said happily, thinking he meant as a special guest—you know, one of those who gives the quick, "Come on, guys, we can do this!" kind of pep talk. Was I ever wrong! Pastor Dennis wanted me to be the featured speaker!

The next weekend I spoke in front of hundreds of men, my knees shaking the entire time. I called my message, "Leaving a Legacy: How to Do It" and shared the same thing I'd explored with the men in my lunch group: how to leave behind a legacy of faith, hope, and love that can impact the lives of your family for generations to come. I gave two messages on Friday night, three on Saturday morning, and at the end of the conference I asked for a show of hands of who might want to continue on this journey called Letters From Dad.

Almost every man raised his hand.

Pastor Dennis was so pumped he asked me to take the pulpit for both Sunday morning services to see if I could get the rest of the men in the congregation to follow suit. That next morning, as I began to teach and share from the pulpit, God performed a mighty work. The hearts of those men were moved, and by the time I finished, more men from the church came forward and chose to be a part of Letters From Dad.

"To All the World . . ."

What had happened at Parkway Hills Baptist Church started me thinking. If it worked this well with one church, why wouldn't it work for churches all across America? But this presented those of us involved with Letters From Dad with a quandary. We had the organization in place for a citywide ministry, but not a national one, and some critical decisions needed to be made. The most important one was how we would grow the ministry. Other movements like Promise Keepers grew by holding mass rallies with tens of thousands of men in attendance. That had worked for them, but we felt like God was calling on us to retain the intimate feeling of a small group. We also felt God wanted us to work within the local church.

To help me with this and other decisions, I formed an advisory board from my original group of fourteen men. We were all flush with the excitement that comes with starting something new, but we also knew we were at a crossroads regarding some tough choices. Convinced that the local church should be the focus of Letters From Dad, we agreed that the best means to further the ministry was to establish large groups within each church that could then be broken down into smaller ones—our Legacy Groups.

The other thing the board decided was that we should

videotape my portion of Letters From Dad. As pastors and men's ministers examined our curriculum, they felt confident they could present that material, but they also felt they needed a twenty-minute presentation from me explaining the philosophy behind the meetings. Well, Billy Graham I'm not, but I did my best. And since misery loves company, I convinced several of the men who had been telling me their powerful stories to record them as well. I also received permission to use the letters I'd been receiving. Armed with these letters and the video interviews, we finally had a tremendous archive of material that all the Legacy Groups across the nation could draw upon.

All of this was a learning experience for me, but fortunately I had a wonderful group of men behind me, every one of them committed to excellence in everything—from the videotaped seminar, to the leather three-ring binders the men kept their personal copies of their letters in, to the letterhead and the stationery they used, to the boxes they gave to their loved ones. When you do something with excellence, I truly believe God blesses it. And He did. Just one short year earlier, we could never have imagined the truly amazing thing that happened next.

The world came calling.

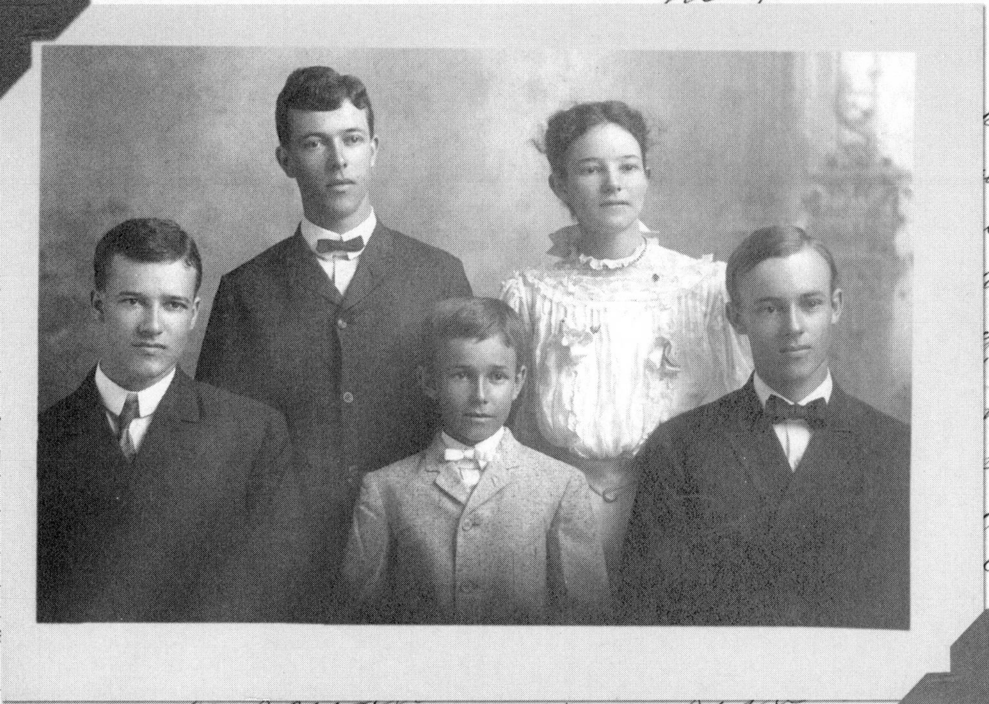

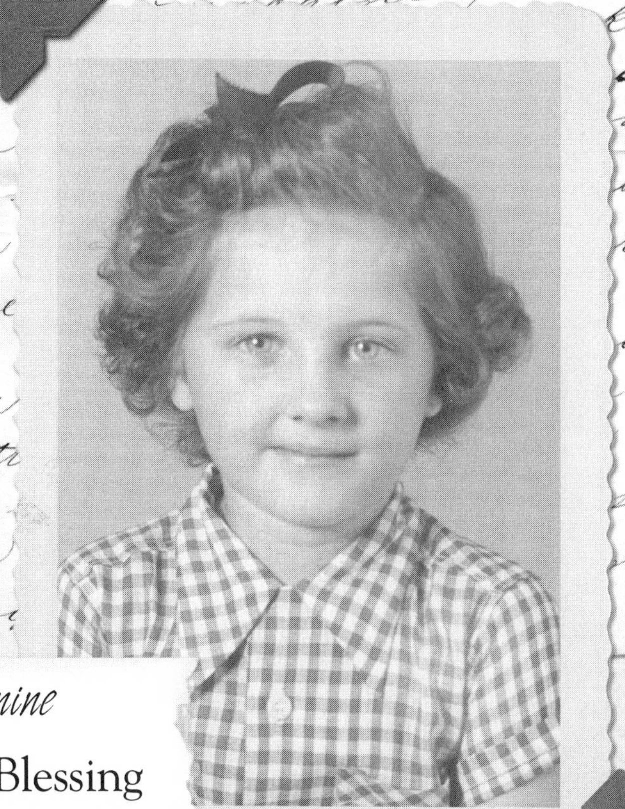

chapter twenty-nine

The Heart of the Blessing

What is God's picture of the future for us? It's eternity with Him.

*H*ave you ever met someone with such a magnetic personality that you just wanted to be around him all the time? That's how I felt the first time I met Pastor Sam Dennis of Parkway Hills Baptist Church.

I'll never forget the first time we met. The chairman of his deacon board asked if we could have lunch and discuss bringing Letters From Dad to their church. As we entered the restaurant, we were greeted by the maitre d', a man who spoke with a heavy foreign accent.

In the blink of an eye, Pastor Dennis was placing his hand on this man's shoulder and saying, "Sir, I don't believe I've had the opportunity to meet you. My name is Sam Dennis. This is the fourth time I've been here, and I want to tell you how impressed I am with how you treat everyone who walks in your doors. You always greet them with a smile and a word of kindness. I think the owner of this place should give you a big raise, and if he's here, I'll tell him so myself."

Talk about making someone's day! The maitre d' was smiling like he'd just won the lottery.

"And by the way," Sam added, "I'm the pastor of a church down the street, and we'd love to have you be our special guest. If you'll come, I'd be honored to have you and your family sit with me and my family."

As I watched this unfold, I was completely dumbfounded. Pastor Dennis had just demonstrated all the parts of a biblical blessing—and he probably didn't even know he'd done it!

I certainly wasn't familiar with how you blessed someone when I first started Letters From Dad. But determined to discover the practical steps of how to do it, I searched

Scripture, beginning with the Old Testament. That was good since that's where the idea of a blessing began. Abraham, Isaac, and Jacob all gave blessings to their families. One of the greatest and most powerful blessings was reserved for the first-born of the family. Remember when Jacob stole Esau's birthright in Genesis 27? That birthright was bestowed by their father, Isaac, in the form of a blessing. This blessing came in two parts: a benediction (verse 28) and a prediction (verse 29).

First, the benediction:

"May God give you of heaven's dew and of earth's rich-ness—an abundance of grain and new wine."

Then the prediction:

"May nations serve you and peoples bow down to you. Be lord over your brothers, and may the sons of your mother bow down to you. May those who curse you be cursed and those who bless you be blessed."

It's also worth noting that this blessing was irreversible. When Esau discovered Jacob's deceit, he asked his father for another blessing. But Isaac replied, "I have made him lord over you and have made all his relatives his servants, and I have sustained him with grain and new wine. So what can I possibly do for you, my son?"(verse 37).

No discussion of the word *blessing* would be complete without looking at Psalm 103:2-5, where we're given the bene-fits of the blessing that God has bestowed upon each of us: "Praise the LORD, O my soul, and forget not all his benefits—who forgives all your sins and heals all your diseases, who redeems your life from the pit and crowns you with love and compassion, who satisfies your desires with good things so that your youth is renewed like the eagle's."

The Four Components of the Blessing

My investigation into the heart of the blessing also took me back to Gary Smalley and John Trent's wonderful book, *The Blessing*. Gary and John broke down the blessing into five components, but for simplicity's sake, I combined two of them. To illustrate each component, I used the points of the cross, since it was the cross that was the ultimate sign of God's blessing on us.

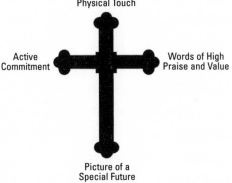

1. Physical Touch—Perhaps no one has demonstrated physical touch so poignantly as Michelangelo in his beautiful painting, "The Creation of Adam."

The fingers from heaven and from earth reach out to each other. God loves to touch us. He came to earth to touch the lepers, the blind, those with demons—all the hurting and suffering people of the world. When Christ interacted with His disciples, He was always touching them. So if this is how God demonstrates affection, should we not do the same? Got a problem with physically holding your kids? Get over it, because that's how God, our Father, showed us how He loved us.

2. Words of High Praise and Value—The second component of the blessing is to use words of high praise and value when addressing the person you want to bless. When Jesus was baptized, God the Father declared words of high value. He boomed down from heaven, "You are My beloved Son, in whom I am well pleased" (Mark 1:11 NKJV). Notice God didn't take Jesus aside and whisper quietly, "Hey, You did good!" No,

God Himself yelled it out in public.

Want to bless your kids? Grab a megaphone and climb to the top of the highest mountain, calling out for all to hear, "You, my children, are blessed! You are the treasures of my life! And I will never leave you nor forsake you!"

But let me toss in a cautionary note. Remember the old children's rhyme, "Sticks and stones may break my bones, but words will never hurt me"? That's not true. Just as words of high value bless those who hear them, words meant to demean curse them. People, especially children, rise to the expectation placed upon them. Expect failure and you'll get failure. Do not—and I can't say this strongly enough—DO NOT say derogatory things to those you love. They are the treasures of your life.

And words matter.

3. Picture of a Special Future—What is God's picture of the future for us? It's eternity with Him. From the beginning of time, He's had the image of spending eternity with us ingrained in His mind. And what a picture that is! God sees it in cinemascope and Technicolor! It's the ultimate family portrait.

When it comes to those you love, paint the same kind of hope-filled picture. As you envision this future, think of your loved one's gifts and talents, so that you can say, "Sweetheart, you will be a great _____" . . . then fill in the blank. Name it, say it, visualize it for that person. Will they be a great doctor, a great mom, a great scientist? Whatever it is, picture it. Do this, then watch them migrate to greatness.

Why? Because you gave them a vision of the future.

4. Active Commitment—The final component of the blessing is what I call "A/C"—Active Commitment. God is actively committed to us. Every day when we wake up, He gives

us breath. Every day He gives us food. He's always there when we need Him. He never forsakes us. And every day of our life He's bringing us a little closer to His kingdom. So what does that mean to us as fathers? What does it mean to be actively committed? For one thing, it means you keep your word. It reminds me of a promise I made to my kids one time when they were little.

The Fourth of July was approaching, and the kids were asking if they could pop firecrackers.

"Sure, no problem," I said, but I didn't take them to buy the firecrackers.

So all week long they came and asked, "Can we buy our fireworks today, Dad?"

And every day I'd say the same thing: "Sure, we'll do that— maybe tomorrow."

The Fourth of July came and guess who hadn't bought firecrackers? Mr. Procrastinator! There I was on the morning of the Fourth, desperately searching the Internet, the Yellow Pages, anywhere I could look to find some place to buy firecrackers. There were no places anywhere near Dallas, but I did succeed in finding a wholesaler in a nearby city. So I loaded the kids in the van and we drove there and ended up buying a boatload of fireworks.

If you were to ask my kids today for a funny story about growing up, each and every one of them would recount that story.

"Poor old Dad, racing all over Texas trying to buy us firecrackers."

But if you were to ask them the point of that story, guess what they'd say?

"My dad keeps his word."

I may have been a little slow in keeping it, but I kept it. I was actively committed to them.

I still am.

The Whole Blessing

When Pastor Dennis spoke to the maitre d', he wasn't just engaging in pastorspeak. He wasn't just being nice for the sake of being nice. He was truly giving a blessing. How? First, he demonstrated physical touch by placing his hand on the maitre d's shoulder when he greeted him. Remember, love is always communicated through the power of touch. Sam then reeled off so many words of high value and praise that I couldn't count them all. He followed that up by presenting a picture of a special future for the maitre d' as he offered to speak to the restaurant's manager about giving the maitre d' a raise. Finally, Sam communicated his active commitment by asking the maitre d' to be his special guest at church.

I think it's safe to say the next time Sam Dennis walks in the door of that restaurant, the maitre d' will remember him and that special blessing he was given.

His true blessing is reserved for those who fear, honor, revere, and obey Him. When you do those things, you change.

*H*ave you ever had a Pastor Dennis in your life? If you have, I'll bet he or she utilized the Four Components of the Blessing—and maybe, like him, without even knowing. I truly believe that you can't be a successful friend, husband, father, mother, grandfather, grandmother, employer, employee, or pastor without instituting these tools in the lives of those around you. In fact, I don't believe you can be a successful anything without using these tools. Everyone responds to a blessing correctly given.

Notice I said "correctly given." If someone sneezes and you say, "God bless you," that's really not the kind of blessing we're talking about here. It's polite, but not very life-changing. Or what about the rapper who stands on the stage at some awards show and says, "I'd like to thank God for all His blessings on me. I got me a recording contract, a huge crib, and some expensive wheels!" Is that God's idea of a blessing? No. God's real blessings change lives from the inside out. His true blessing is reserved for those who fear, honor, revere, and obey Him. When you do those things, you change. You begin caring for others and taking care of them.

Just like Pastor Dennis.

And when you become like that, you'll discover what it means to be truly blessed.

Have You Had Your Blessing Today?

I know I have! I am humbled by all the blessings I've received from family and friends, but most importantly from my heavenly Father. He has taken a broken-down, middle-aged man and given him a new purpose in life. In one sixty-day period, while being inundated with requests from Christian schools and churches from across the nation to come teach my course, I received the offer to write this book. Me! The Shakespeare of bathroom walls!

During that time I also got phone calls from prison chaplains asking me to make Letters From Dad available to the prison system. And on top of that, some of the nation's largest corporations started calling, asking me to come speak. But by far the most surprising call I received was from a chaplain at the Pentagon who asked me to make Letters From Dad available to the military.

"It's changed my life," he told me over the phone. "I've always had a great relationship with my wife and kids, but now it's even better! And now as I walk the halls of the Pentagon, I'm like a man on a mission, seeking out people I can bless!"

Why all this interest from secular America? Actually, it's an easy answer: because relationships matter, whether they're in the marketplace, the military, or a prison. The principles of a blessing strengthen every relationship in every setting. When you look at the attributes of God, the one that attracts people the most is love. Everyone responds to it. And when you bless your employees, your employer, your co-workers, or your peers, you're showering them with love. It was love that motivated God to shower us with the greatest blessing of all: His Son, Jesus Christ.

And now God was giving me the opportunity to take this truth into the secular world in a whole new way.

The Timeline of Your Life

One of the speaking engagements I accepted during this time was to the executives of a major corporation. I began that speech by telling those busy men about the time line of their lives.

As I spoke to the executives of that corporation, I told them that everything that had taken place in their lives before that night was irrelevant because the rest of their lives began right then.

"The first question you have to ask yourself is, 'Where am I on that timeline?'" I offered. "And if you're like me and you're edging toward the end, then the next question you have to ask yourself is, 'Where am I going when this life is over?'"

At that point, I presented the gospel and described how the ultimate blessing of God is the Cross, using Acts 16:31 as my key verse: "Believe in the Lord Jesus, and you will be saved—you and your household."

As I was presenting this, I noticed a prominent businessman sitting on the front row. He was a leader of tens of thousands of men and women in the insurance industry. There's usually no one harder to reach with the gospel than a successful businessman, and yet his eyes seemed riveted on me. I offered up a quick, silent prayer, asking God to touch this man's heart. Then before I closed my presentation, I said to all the men present, "Guys, I just showed you how brief your time is upon this planet, so before I let you go, I would be remiss if I didn't ask you one final question: Have you received the greatest blessing of all? Have you received the blessing of the Cross—the free gift of salvation?"

I followed that by leading them in a simple prayer. As I finished, I told the men to keep their eyes closed.

"Did anyone pray that prayer?" I asked.

As I scanned the audience, I saw that businessman's hand go up. I've heard of people's hearts leaping for joy, but mine almost leapt off that podium and dragged me along with it! I closed the session and asked the men to move into their Legacy Groups. When they did, this businessman told his group he'd just accepted Christ. They immediately surrounded him and welcomed him into God's kingdom.

But the story doesn't end there. Only a month later, this same businessman called and asked if I would be willing to share the Four Components of the Blessing at a large regional conference where many of his sales staff would be assembled.

It's experiences like these that have affirmed God's plan with this ministry—one that's bigger than I could've ever imagined. With the universal message of Letters From Dad, God can truly use these principles to touch the hearts of anyone.

*I truly believe with all my
heart that the winds of
Malachi 4:6 are blowing.*

Three thousand years ago, thirty thousand men danced upon a hill. Thirty thousand men celebrating the return of the ark of the covenant to the children of Israel. We've already talked about what was inside this box: the Ten Commandments. God's first letter to mankind.

But that's not all. There was also a golden jar containing manna and Aaron's rod which sprouted buds—keepsakes for the Jewish people. These were markers of their past, just as your Memory Box will contain a record of your memories, your traditions, and your legacy to future generations. Someday, when your great-grandchildren ask your grandchildren, "Tell me about Great-Granddad," they'll be able to open their Memory Box . . . and you'll be there.

Reconciliation

Remember Jim Canton, the man who had been through a difficult divorce and hadn't heard from his kids in five years? The man who had almost given up on ever seeing his children again? After Jim sent his boxes to his kids, two years went by without a word. Then, only a few months ago at one of our Legacy meetings, Jim came running up to me with a big smile on his face.

"Greg, you'll never believe what happened! Last week my daughter looked up on the shelf in her closet and saw the mahogany box I'd sent her. She took it down, opened the letter, and read it for the first time. Then she called me and said, 'Dad, this foolishness has got to stop.' She wants to see me! My baby wants to see me!"

It's just a beginning. There are still some wounds to be

healed. But we serve a great God, and they will be healed. When people ask me why I got involved in Letters From Dad, I point to men like Jim Canton and say, "Because I'm just a starving beggar who stumbled into a warehouse of more food than I can possibly eat. And so I'm going out telling other beggars, 'Hey, come on in, let's eat!'"

I truly believe with all my heart that the winds of Malachi 4:6 are blowing. The warm wind of the Spirit of God is melting the hearts of men, turning "the hearts of the fathers to their children, and the hearts of the children to their fathers."

Lift your hand up high. Feel the wind? I hope so. I pray it is blowing in and through your heart today!

"Send Me Someone to Bless!"

My wife and I were in the Pacific Northwest recently helping some local churches start their own Letters From Dad groups when some friends of Carolyn's invited us to dinner. These were the people who had led Carolyn to the Lord and with whom she had gone to Bible school. She was excited about seeing them, and so she declared that such a special occasion called for a special dress. (Of course it did. Why didn't I think of that?)

We made a beeline to her favorite dress shop, and as we walked in the door, I noticed a middle-aged saleswoman folding clothes and tidying up. What drew my attention to her was how happy she seemed in her work, and so I asked her if she could help us.

"It would be my honor to serve you," she said. Not your normal response from a salesperson in today's retail world.

Carolyn found something she liked and went into the dressing room to try it on. When she reemerged wearing a stunning pants suit, I remarked to the saleswoman, "Wow, doesn't she look beautiful?"

To which the saleswoman replied, "Sir, you are truly blessed." Once again, not the usual words I'm accustomed to hearing from a salesperson.

Carolyn settled on the pants suit, and as we were paying, I said to the saleswoman, "Ma'am, I was impressed by the words you used a moment ago."

Immediately I saw her eyes dance with excitement as if some secret code had been broken.

"Sir, I spoke those words to you because I know Jesus. He is the Lord of my life. Do you know Him?"

Surprised by her bold witness, I declared, "Why yes. Yes, I do."

With passion in her voice, she boldly declared, "This morning I asked the Lord to send me someone whom I could bless. May I give you the blessing I believe the Lord has for you today?"

How could I refuse? And I'll never forget her words, spoken without a moment's hesitation. "Sir, I pray the oil of God's blessing over your life, that it will flow upon your head like the oil Samuel poured over the head of David as he anointed him the future king over Israel."

"Wow!" was all I could say when she was done. But then fortunately I remembered to thank her. "And may God bless you in the same way!" Then we went our separate ways, never to see each other again on this side of God's kingdom.

Was I to be a future king over anything? No. But the spirit of her blessing made me king for a day. For a week! As a matter of fact, I still feel that blessing. It was God speaking through her to remind me of His great love for me and of His great desire to pour out His blessings over my life.

It took a lot of courage for her to do that. But then, she serves a courageous God.

Free Blessings

I trust the reason you've continued reading this book is that you, too, wish to bestow such a blessing upon another. God bless you for that. And I pray you won't let one more heartbeat go by before doing so.

So where will you start? Who in your life needs a blessing today? Is it a son or daughter, a parent or grandparent, your wife, your pastor, your boss, your neighbor, or your best friend? Could it be that stranger sitting next to you on the bus or subway? Could it be the man sitting in a lonely jail cell without any hope?

No matter who it is, be bold as you pour out God's blessing over their life. And give it freely, my friend. Give it freely.

Just as it was freely given to you.

WESTERN UNION TELEGRAM

chapter thirty-two

My Mother's Cedar Chest

The most wonderful blessing a father ever bestowed upon his children is the one our heavenly Father bestowed upon us all: the gift of eternal life through His Son, Jesus Christ.

I never received my father's blessing.

But I did receive my heavenly Father's blessing: eternal life through His Son, Jesus Christ. In the final analysis, that's all that really matters. And that wasn't the only miracle God performed in my life. He used the absence of my earthly father's blessing as the impetus to begin what's become a worldwide ministry. Only He could come up with such a plan.

But my story wouldn't be complete without relating to you one final incident in this journey called Letters From Dad.

Memories Unlocked

In all the time that Letters From Dad has been going on now, there has only been one woman ever allowed into a Legacy Group.

You guessed it: my mom.

I'll never forget her comment as we drove home after that meeting.

"I've never seen anything like that. Someone would have to see it to believe it."

A few weeks later, I was visiting her at my boyhood home in Lubbock when she suddenly said, "Son, that night I was at Letters From Dad and you told all those people how badly you wanted your father's signature . . . well, that got me to thinking. Come here a minute."

And like a little boy who'd gotten himself into trouble, I followed Mom into her room.

"Sit down, son. There's something I want to show you."

Now, as I've told you, my mother is in poor health. So there I was, surrounded by oxygen equipment, walkers, and canes as

I watched her teeter over to an old cedar chest and kneel down.

Mom had had that chest as long as I could remember. I'd once stolen a peek when I was a boy, and I could still remember the musty cedar smell that had greeted me when I'd opened it. But as it held no toys, my curiosity was short-lived, and I hadn't thought of it since. Now my mom was about to open it again, and I found myself racking my brain trying to remember what I'd seen inside that chest so many years before. Images of paper and cloth came to mind, but certainly nothing of my father's.

So what could it be?

Picture that room for a moment. Small, dimly lit. Ornate frames filled with family pictures on tables and hanging from walls. Late afternoon sunlight filtering through venetian blinds. And my mom lifting the lid of that great cedar chest.

And then it happened . . . the scent of cedar flooded the room. In an instant, I was a small boy again, kneeling on scabby knees beside that chest, breathing in that smell.

How is it that a fragrance can magically transport you back to childhood like a time machine? Fresh mown grass always brings back memories of warm summer nights catching fireflies in mason jars. And blue spruce! One sniff and my mind is awash with the glitter and joy of Christmas.

But the smell of cedar . . . ah, that one is special. At least for me. For somewhere within its mysterious fragrance exists my mom, captured still in all her youth and beauty.

It was with childish eyes that I watched her rummage through that chest until she suddenly stopped and slowly lifted something out. In her weathered hands she held a packet of old, tattered letters wrapped with worn-out twine.

There was a glistening in my mom's eyes as she turned to me and said, "Son, what you don't know is that while your father was overseas during World War II, he was a prolific letter writer. And here are just sixty of the letters he wrote me."

Then she handed them to me as the tears came in earnest. "These are yours, son. These are yours."

I took them, holding them like a father holds his newborn. And the first thing I noticed was my dad's signature, "Earl E. Vaughn," in the upper left-hand corner of the envelope.

God had given me my father's signature.

I poured through those letters over the next few days as if my life depended on it. Here was my father, a man who could never say the words "I love you"

to me, saying those words—writing those words—to my mom. In one poignant letter, he said he had prayed that someday they'd have four boys. And that's exactly what God gave him. Four boys. Although these letters weren't written to me, through them I discovered the heart of my father, and they made me realize something. My father had given me his blessing—in his own way.

Acceptance

Toward the end of his life, my dad was experiencing fourth-stage Alzheimer's when we finally had to place him in a nursing home. It was a nice facility out in the countryside that he loved so much. Not long before he died, I sat with him on the porch of the nursing home. We didn't speak much, as the silences are fairly long in a conversation with an Alzheimer's patient. In fact, at that point Dad rarely spoke at all and could remember very little.

As we sat there in silence, I had a chance to think back over my life with my father. The bad times were quickly forgotten as many wonderful memories flooded my mind—family vacations and Christmases and fishing trips. Without even thinking about it, I turned to Dad as if he were still the man he used to be and said, "Hey Dad, remember that time we were fishing in Arkansas and you caught that enormous fish? How big was that fish?"

As soon as I said it, I chastised myself. *What are you doing? He doesn't remember.*

You can imagine my shock when my father's face lit up with a grin from ear to ear and he said with true fisherman's pride, "Twenty pounds!"

Dad died a few weeks later.

No, I never got my hug, or my "I love you," or my "I'm proud of you, son." But what I did get was the best my father could give. I got a nice house to grow up in with food in the pantry, a car in the driveway, and a college education. I got a warm coat in the winter, fresh tennis shoes in the summer, and a nice suit to wear to Sunday school.

Would I have traded them all for a hug? In a New York minute.

But it was the best my father could do, and I accept it.

No, I cherish it.

And for those of you who are wondering if I ever wrote my dad a letter of tribute, I did.

You're reading it.

I love you, Dad, and someday I'm going to get that hug . . . when we meet again in a better place.

CLASS OF SERVICE		1201	SYMBOLS

WESTERN UNION

This is a full-rate Telegram or Cable-gram unless its de-ferred character is in-dicated by a suitable symbol above or pre-ceding the address.

DL=Day Letter
NT=Overnight Telegram
LC=Deferred Cable
NLT=Cable Night Letter
Ship Radiogram

A. N. WILLIAMS
PRESIDENT

NEWCOMB CARLTON
CHAIRMAN OF THE BOARD

J. C. WILLEVER
FIRST VICE-PRESIDENT

The filing time shown in the date line on telegrams and day letters is STANDARD TIME at point of origin. Time of receipt is STANDARD TIME at point of destination

D294 9=WUX DENVER COLO 16 326P

MISS WANDA NELSON=   1943 JAN 16 PM 5 12

2307 7 ST

MY HEART AT HALF MAST UNTIL YOU FULLY RECOVER=

EARL

THE COMPANY WILL APPRECIATE SUGGESTIONS FROM ITS PATRONS CONCERNING ITS SERVICE

The Father's Blessing

There is a truth to be learned in Letters From Dad. It's really quite simple. A father's blessing is a wonderful gift. But the most wonderful blessing a father ever bestowed upon his children is the one our heavenly Father bestowed upon us all: the gift of eternal life through His Son, Jesus Christ.

It's a gift that heals all wounds, brings joy amid pain, and conquers death.

It is His gift to me, and to you.

And it is the greatest blessing of all.

S/Sgt Earl Va...
2nd Tech Sch...
Lowry Fed C...
PO...

CORRESPON...

Dear Wanda,

This writin...
may not be le...
as I am tryin...
write between...
Did you get...
card? Write m...
6 days becau...
am moving...
Monday. Lo...
Lovee...

S/Sgt Ea...
2nd Tech Sch...
Lowry Field,...

Hi...

Miss Wanda Nelson,
2307-7th Strut,
Lubbock, Texas

...bed with no one
bother me. You know, the life of Raleigh!
...an't you envy me? Hon, it is days like

The following are actual letters. The writers have graciously allowed us to publish these in hopes they will be of benefit to you as you write your own letters.

Letter to a Spouse

Dearest Karen,

When I was a little boy, one of my favorite ways to start the weekend was to get up early on Saturday to watch cartoons and eat a big plate full of hot pancakes smothered with melted butter and plenty of Vermont Maid Syrup. I clearly remember that the syrup bottle had a green label with a picture of a smiling pretty girl who had two braids of shoulder-length brown hair. I also remember carefully studying that green label and wondering about that mysterious attractive girl as I downed each sweet mouthful of breakfast. Little did I know that I would someday meet, fall in love with, and marry my own real live Vermont maid complete with a bright smile, two braids of shoulder-length brown hair, and kisses sweeter than any maple syrup!

Wow, you are a real dream come true! I know exactly how Adam felt when God presented Eve to Him and he exclaimed, "At last! You are flesh of my flesh and bone of my bones!" Karen, you complete my life. With God at the center of our marriage, we can face whatever life throws our way. As I promised in my wedding vows, "The storms of life can blow and blow, but they won't knock me down. We'll stand the test, the test of time, 'cause we stand on holy ground."

We've definitely had our share of storms, but I want you to know that I will stand right by your side, whatever comes our way. Since I love to sing, I can't help but think of how perfectly another song's lyrics echo my feelings: I will be here, and you can cry on my shoulder/When the mirror tells us we're older, I will hold you/And I will be here to watch you grow in beauty/And tell you all the things you are to me/I will be true to the promise I have made/To you and the One who gave you to me.[1]

I look forward to growing old with you and experiencing life together. I love you with all my heart. You are a gift from God—my best friend and the love of my life.

Forever yours,
Ted

Letter to a Child

Dear _____,

The box that contained this is a small Christmas gift to you to hold cards and letters from the people who love you. In the coming months and years I want to write down in words what is in my heart and also pass along some fatherly wisdom in what I'm calling "Letters From Dad." My prayer is that these letters will be kept in this box and be of value to you someday, and that you in turn will do this for your future children. I believe the pleasures of letter writing have faded in my generation and may be forgotten in your generation.

The following is a true account of an event that I want to share with you.

Strength from Disaster

In the early 1990s, several men and women entered a glass dome environment called the Biosphere for a period of two years to test the concept of living on other planets in self-sustained atmospheres. Months after the doors were sealed, an unexpected thing happened in the dome's forest, designed to supply oxygen to the residents. One by one, the trees began to bend over and split in half. Scientists soon discovered the reason for the forest's demise. It was because there was no wind under the dome. You see, as trees grow they depend on the wind to whip the limbs back and forth, thereby producing microscopic cracks in the bark. As the cracks heal, they help to strengthen the entire tree. Without the menacing wind and continual lesions in the bark, whole trees eventually toppled over and died.

We too depend on the winds of life to push us to and fro, for it is pain and sorrow in our lives that help strengthen us, building a strong Christian character. James 1:12 says, "Blessed is the man who perseveres under trial, because when he has stood the test, he will receive the crown of life that God has promised to those who love him."

As I look back over the last six years that we have been physically separated, I see so many areas as your dad that I could have done better. I have hurt you deeply and have made lots of mistakes and pray that you have forgiven me. But more than that, I want you to know that I love you unconditionally, which means that no matter what happens, my love will never diminish for you. I will always want the best for you and be proud to call you my daughter.

From the few times that we have talked, I know that you are living a full life and your priorities are in the right places. It is obvious that you are doing fine without my advice, but as I grow older and more reflective, I have a need to communicate to you what I believe are important lessons I have learned through my life experiences. I just ask that you read my letters with memories of good times we spent together and with an open heart.

I want to close this first letter with some fatherly advice and my blessing to you. Aim for perfection, be an encouragement to others, test everything, and hold on to what is good. May the grace of Jesus Christ, the love of God, and the fellowship of the Holy Spirit be with you through a joyous Christmas season.

All my love,
Dad

Letter to a Grandchild

(Just in case I can't be there ...)
My Dear and Precious Michael Hayden:

It's Christmas. Your first Christmas. And I wanted to share a few thoughts with you on this wonderful day.

First, I'd like to confess something to you. I often wondered why people got so excited about having grandchildren. For me, life was more than filled with the joy and demands of raising seven children. At the time of this letter, I still have four children in college and the thought of another child was, shall I say, overwhelming. The day of your birth was such a big event. I felt like a spectator at a big football game, as there were more than fifteen people in the delivery room.

A strange thing happened only fourteen days after your birth. Your mom and dad called and asked if we would be able to keep you over the weekend. You were so very small, and you slept in our bedroom. I knew that I wouldn't get a wink of sleep because your Grandmother Carolyn would be up every ten minutes to see if you were still breathing, so I decided to sleep upstairs. About 5:00 in the morning, I was awakened by the screams of a very hungry Michael Hayden, so I came downstairs to find your grandmother preparing a bottle. As I looked at your exhausted grandmother, I suggested that I give you the bottle and for her to get some sleep. Believe me, she needed it!

And then it happened. As Carolyn placed you in my arms, I looked into your eyes and saw something I've never seen before. The very face of my loving God. There He was looking at me through your eyes. As you took your first bottle from your grandfather, you were mine and I was yours. I have never felt anything like this, even with my own children. After you finished your bottle you looked up at me in total peace and contentment. As you rested in my arms, I placed my big hand on your tiny head and prayed a blessing over your life.

"Lord, this is my Michael Hayden. He is Your child. He is to be a joy to his family and a joy to You. I claim this young boy as a servant of the Most High God. I proclaim that he will be a blessing to his family, but more importantly a blessing to You. I pledge to him my unwavering love, prayer, and encouragement. I commit to be the kind of grandfather that will make him proud. I pray that he will come to know You at an early age and will follow You all the days of his life. I picture for him a special future of service, and I pledge my lifelong love to him. Amen."

Those were the moments I fell in love with you. As I reflected on this prayer, I realized that I had assumed something that might not be true: I assumed that I would live to see this happen. And that, my son, is a wrong assumption. I began to think of a way to leave you and the other members of our family some Christmas love gifts, just in case I can't be there. So this Christmas I wanted to give this gift to you as a sample of what I'm calling "Christmas Time Capsules." I will see that for the next ten years, after I'm gone to be with Jesus, that you and the rest of the family will have a special gift under the tree from me. I have asked your aunt Becky to see that you and the family receive these gifts from me.

Though you can't understand all this now, I pray that someday you'll remember that you had a Grandfather Greg who loved and prayed for you all the days of your life.

Blessing to you, my grandson,
Gregory Lee Vaughn

Letter of Tribute

Dear Dad,

I write these words to you and now speak them into existence this morning in the presence of family and friends who have come to honor you. These words are for you, but I openly repeat them in this great sanctuary before this diverse group of people to give my testimony, to be a witness of what I know, and to make a public record of what you mean to me.

Daddy, husband, father, Dad, son, brother, Grandy to your grandchildren, Rev. _____, Brother _____, playmate, mentor, sponsor, pastor, preacher, coach, cheerleader, supporter, evangelist, sportsman, great speaker, missionary, educated, highly intelligent, athlete, accomplished musician, counselor, funny, fun-loving, disciplined, integrity, character, truth, love, honesty, humility, aggressive, strong-willed, determined, courageous, committed, simple, and full of class are only a few of the words available to me in any language I know that describe you and your qualities.

This past Tuesday we stood at the threshold of the door of a transition so significant that only you and I know to what degree, and only the future will bear out. Today we walk through this door of transition as we place your physical body in the earth for the time being. There is so much I want to say in these few brief moments, so I will only touch on the highlights.

What a man you were! You were the kind of father who would stand by your son no matter what I was up to. I'll never forget my first jury trial at the mature age of twenty, five years before I would receive my law degree and license to practice law. I was caught speeding in a school zone near the house. I protested my guilt, proclaimed my innocence, and demanded a jury trial in the little municipal court of the town of Buckingham. I got my jury trial and violated a cardinal rule that I would later learn: "He who represents himself has a fool for a client."

I called you as a witness and asked you if you had ever seen me speeding. Notwithstanding the fact that the question was improper under the rules of evidence, I knew your answer would be no—and it was, because I tried my best not to let you ride with me in my car since I knew you would not approve of my driving habits. I knew what you were thinking, but you wouldn't say it. You were thinking, *Son, what a foolish thing to do. You're guilty and you know it. Take your lumps and move on.* But no, you kept silent and let me learn the lesson, all the while standing at my side in support. It was the fastest guilty verdict in history—less than three minutes, as I recall. But you humored me, and we laughed together later in the parking lot of the little portable building that was the courthouse.

In going through old papers and files at the house, Mom came across the budget you prepared for your honeymoon. Really, Dad, you typed up a budget and presented it to Mom for her consideration in planning your honeymoon forty years ago. I mean, you had the exact mileage calculated as to how far you would drive, gas prices, oil change, food, etc. You were such a tightwad. In honor of this trait, we want you to know that we decided to save money on your funeral, so we opted for the wooden box. (Just kidding, Dad. It was more expensive than most of the steel and stainless steel models.)

But seriously, when people think about death, many think only in terms of finite things handed down, such as an inheritance of assets and the like. You have left these behind, but oh, there are many other things that you leave behind to me, such as the genes and chromosomes in my body that make me look like you, my strong will and determination that come in part from you, my fearlessness in the face of adversity, and the will to press forward, dream dreams, and accomplish goals.

But Dad, the most important thing that you have handed down to me is your faith. Years ago, as I sat and listened to you share your faith, you taught me of a Man Who was born in an obscure village, Who worked in a carpenter shop until He was thirty, Who then became an itinerant preacher. He never held an office. He never had a family or owned a house. He didn't go to college. He had no credentials but Himself. All the armies that ever marched, all the navies that ever sailed, all the parliaments that ever sat, and all the kings that ever reigned have not affected the life of man on this earth as much as He. Nineteen centuries have come and gone, and today He is the central figure of the human race and His name is Jesus Christ, the Son of God.

Next to Him, Dad, I want you to know that you stand as the most significant man in my life. Medical science says you shouldn't have lasted the four years after you suffered your stroke in 1992. But you did, and during that time you taught us so much. You carried around a body that limited you in function, but not once did you complain. You lived on a higher spiritual plane, not one chained to the complexities of our physical lives and busy daily activities that consume the seconds, minutes, and hours of every day. You showed us joy in the simple three things of life: being together, sharing together, and loving each other and our fellow man.

Love. It's a word that is so misunderstood and branded onto so many things. There's a song, Dad, where the writer penned these words that in part sum up what I received from you in the last four years. It goes like this:

> *When it comes to love, I'd do most anything/'Cause if you have it in your heart you know you're a rich man/There's just not enough, to go around the world today/And if we had a little more you know it'd be a better place/I can only go by what's happened to me/And now I realize when it comes to love/You're gonna cry a little, hurt a little, feel a little pain in your heart/Laugh a little, care a lot, take a look at what you've got/It's true we're human, we make mistakes, but we're gonna live to see a brighter day/So do what you gotta do/When it comes to love, I just wanna have it all/It's not something you can buy in any store/Someone to trust—that's what I'm lookin' for/I'm gonna open up my heart and ask you to open yours/I'm not tryin' to tell you how it should be/I just want to show you clearly, when it comes to love.*[2]

The love of God lit up your life and body like a lighthouse beacon. You are a rich man, Dad. Thank you for blazing the trail. Thank you for setting the standard. Thank you for making it all clear. Thank you for pointing me to the God of the cross of Calvary as my only source of hope and strength. Thank you for the living example that you were and that your memory will be. In business parlance, Dad, you were the best chairman of the board and chief executive officer that anyone would ever want or need for their family. In an age where role models are lacking, I want you to know you're my champion and hero.

Today I honor you in spoken words. My life's desire is to honor you in my daily life and actions by emulating your example for my own wife and children, so that one day, God willing, Cathy, Andrew, Caroline, and Alexa will say the same of me. I cry tears in recognition of the loss of you, but I celebrate the faith that gives me hope and the knowledge that you are in heaven above, leaving your death with no sting and your grave with no victory. You should know that in your death I am forever changed and different. As the songwriter wrote, "I'm gonna do what I gotta do." And so I do not say good-bye because you are not in this room. But I say to you: I'll see you soon at the end of the course you so carefully and unselfishly marked. Thank you for leading the way. Thank you for fathering me. I proudly bear your name.

I adore you, and most of all I love you, Dad.

Your Son

P.S. I intend to complete much of the work you started, helping people who cannot help themselves and sharing the faith you handed down to me.

Letter of Blessing to a Parent

Dear Dad,

Today I want to give you a blessing . . .

I am blessed to have a dad like you who loved and cared for me. (Thank You, Lord, for giving me a wonderful dad.)

I am blessed to have a dad who has loved his wife and remained faithful to her.

(I thank God you are not like so many men I have seen over the years who left their wives and kids when things didn't go "their way." Thanks for hanging in there during the tough times!)

I am blessed to have a dad who has set an example for me in moral purity.

(I am encouraged to maintain moral purity in my marriage because of your example. I can remember even as a young boy how you did not "check out" other women.)

I am blessed to have a dad who taught me integrity and honesty.

(You have always been fair and honest with people, even when I was the only person who knew about it. I can remember times when it cost you money in your business to charge less and remain true to your word.)

I am blessed to have a dad who taught me to "do it right or don't do it at all."

(From making pinewood derby cars to repairing the cracks in my retaining wall at our house, you always go above and beyond to make sure it is done right the first time.)

I am blessed to have a dad who disciplined me when I needed it.

(I knew better than to talk back to you or act up because you would correct me. All you had to do was look at me a certain way and I knew I had better straighten up. This has helped me be a better father and provide the necessary discipline for my children.)

I am blessed to have a dad who taught me to work hard.

(I will never forget those hot summer days in Nebraska when we learned "good old-fashioned hard work" by loading and stacking hay bales. That work ethic has paid off in sports and throughout life.)

I am blessed to have you as my dad!

Thanks Dad, and may God bless, guide, and direct your path (Psalm 25:4-5).

Final Letter

Farewell, My Dearest Family
May You Finish Strong
May 13, 2003

To my precious family—S, D, N & S

Farewell, My Loved Ones:

I realize few people ever write a "farewell" letter to their loved ones. However, I was reminded this weekend at church as we prayed for three families who had suffered the sudden and unexpected loss of family members that we never know when God might call us home. I want to leave you all with a letter that expresses my thoughts and feelings after I am gone.

First of all, let's talk briefly about the business "stuff." S, you know where the life insurance documents and will are located. You also know what is contained in each in terms of amounts and content. D, N, and S, please honor me and your mother by humbly working together to carry out what is detailed in the will. My desire is to make sure your basic needs are taken care of. The intent was not to provide you with instant wealth and a life of luxury. Rather, my desire is that you would learn to trust God more fully as you grow and mature in your relationship with Him.

S, please know that you are the love of my life. I can't describe the depth of my love for you. It is incredible to see how our love matured from the early years of physical touch and conversation, to communicating by facial expressions and body language, and then to the point of simply knowing what the other person was thinking because of all that we had experienced together. Thank you for your love and devotion to me over the years. You have taught me so much about loyalty and being a servant. Your energy level, organization skills, and drive are second to none. I am convinced you could have easily been the CEO of a company if God had called you to such a position. I am thankful He allowed our family to reap the benefits of your gifts and talents and not a company.

We have had so much fun together as I reflect on our college years and married years. Think about the wonderful trips we have taken together and all that we experienced together in places like Russia, England, Switzerland, and Florida, to mention a few. Wow! Those were the best of times! As I have told you many times, you are not only my wonderful wife and lover, but you have always been my best friend. I trust your judgment completely in moving forward with your life. I have already prayed that God would protect you and grant you the peace and strength to move forward with confidence in making decisions in those areas you trusted me for. I love you S and praise God for blessing me with such a wonderful woman.

D, I hope you always maintain that beautiful and radiant smile. You light up the room with that smile. I want to encourage you in being confident that all things are possible in and through God. I have seen you get stressed over sporting events, cheerleader tryouts, and relationships. Yes, I know part of that is your age and stage of life, and yes, I probably went through the same thing. However, I want to encourage you by learning to trust God each day with each worry and concern. The most important thing is giving it over to Him and having faith He will take care of you.

Please remember the things I have told you about dating, marriage, and purity. I hope you pass these truths on to your sister and brother and to your children. God's plan for marriage is what is best. He wants us to experience incredible joy in our marriage relationships, and this is only possible if we follow His plan of remaining pure. I know it is not easy, but the difficult path is the best and will bring the most joy.

I love you, D, and I have always admired the passion and drive God has blessed you with. You are a great leader, and it has been awesome to see how you have reached out to others who didn't know Christ and were a part of seeing them come to Him as their Savior. Don't ever lose that passion for outreach. It will keep you from getting bogged down with the insignificant things in life. Keep being the social and fun-loving person that you are and that God has gifted you to be. I know you will accomplish great things in your life in whatever you do. I love you.

N, I love you and will miss taking walks with you and talking about all kinds of things and laughing together. I have always loved the way you appreciate God's creation and are interested in science and nature. I also hope you keep the sensitivity you have toward others. You have always been loving and kind to others.

You also have the greatest laugh. From the time you were a little girl I will always remember your laugh. Uncle Mitch always said he missed hearing your laugh when we moved from Cincinnati and how it made him smile each time he thought about your laugh. I have always admired how calm and cool you remain when you are playing sports. Work hard and do your best as you excel in sports, N. I believe God has gifted you in that area and I know you can accomplish great things if you choose to go after it.

Please know that God has a special plan for your life and that He has a special man for you as well. Remember how many times you watched *A Walk to Remember* and how you saw your dad cry when he watched it for the first time? God will honor your obedience with a wonderful husband if you remain pure and wait for the right man. God has demonstrated His faithfulness throughout my life, and I want you to know you can trust Him. Please do your best to get along with your sister and brother. I trust that you all will have great relationships with one another and that you will get along throughout your life. I love you!

Buckskin! Remember how I used to say when you were older and living away from home I was going to call you and greet you by saying "Buckskin"? What a joy it has been for me to have a son as special as you. It has been so much fun for me to laugh and talk to you about sports and to see you develop as a young man. Your athletic ability and competitive fire will serve you well as you grow and mature. It has been a true blessing to see you mature and learn how to lose with grace and dignity. We were thrilled when Allison G told your mother and me how you encouraged Matt and Alex after you lost your basketball game! Way to go, dude! Keep it up!

S, I hope you will continue to grow and mature in your relationship with God. God has been so good to me over the years, and I want you to know that if you learn to trust Him and are obedient to Him, you will live a blessed and content life. It is not about being rich and famous. It is about being humble and learning to trust God, the Creator of this universe. As you pursue your desires and ambitions, please keep God first in your life and follow Him. S, you are so talented. You have a "million-dollar" smile and great looks. You have a great sense of humor, and I know you will be successful. My only concern is that you will take these blessings for granted and that you will not honor God with these gifts that He has given you. I also want you to be faithful to God throughout your dating years. Please honor and respect the girls you date and maintain godly standards in all your relationships. God will honor your obedience in remaining pure before you are married. It will not be easy, but God's best is in store for you and your marriage if you wait. I love you!

Farewell, my loved ones. I can't wait to greet you with a big hug in heaven when you arrive. You know me; I will be asking you to go for a walk so we can "catch up" and enjoy God's creation. Don't worry, I am confident the weather will be perfect and you will never get tired.

Appendix B

Further Insights from Reg Grant on Writing

A Rose by Any Other Name

When you write, employ the senses. We have five major senses. Use them all. You want to show at least as much as you tell. Ask yourself when you come to the end of the paragraph, "Is there anything in this paragraph that I can see, smell, taste, touch, or hear?" You could say, "I love you," or you could say, "My love for you is like a fresh spring day on the Texas prairie. It makes my heart glad." Or you could say, like Romeo to Juliet, "A rose by any other name would smell as sweet." One of the more famous quotes from Shakespeare, right? Everyone's heard it. But what most people don't know is that this line was a veiled swipe by Shakespeare at his rival in the theater business, the Rose Theater, which was known for having less than adequate sanitary conditions. Nevertheless, it has stuck in people's minds for hundreds of years because of its appeal to the senses.

The key point here is to use those senses in your writing because that's how we learn as human beings. If you tell someone something, three hours later they'll only remember about 70 percent of what you said. That sounds pretty good, right? But what happens if you just show them something? No words—you just show them a picture. Three hours later they'll remember about 72 percent of what they were shown. If you combine the two, using both words and pictures, then three hours later they'll retain an amazing 85 percent! That's really good, right?

Watch what happens after three days. For those you only told, their retention rate drops to 10 percent. They've forgotten 90 percent of what you told them. For those you showed something, they'll remember only 20 percent. Better, but if you combine the senses, showing and telling, people will retain 65 percent.

What does this have to do with writing? It tells us that we need to be appealing to as many senses as possible. We learn to do that by taking the time to ask ourselves at the end of every paragraph, "Can I see it, smell it, taste it, touch it, or hear it?" The more we do that, the better people will remember what we wrote.

Clear as Mud

Another helpful hint in writing is to avoid clichés. Avoid them like the plague. They're old hat. And besides that, they don't hold water. I think you get the idea.

Why are clichés so tempting to use? Because they usually relate a concept or an emotion to something visual. Clichés are memorable not only for their catchy phrasing but also for their "visibility." And as we just learned, visual language is one of the most effective tools for unforgettable, impactive writing.

Scientists tell us that the human brain is divided into two halves, the left and right hemispheres. The left side, or left hemisphere, is where we store written language. Number skills are also housed in the left brain. Reasoning is a left-brain function. Spoken language is acquired and kept in the left brain primarily. And the left brain controls your right-side motor function. The left brain is logical, linear, analytical, unemotional, fairly stringent and box-like in its thinking. It's Joe Friday—"Just the facts, ma'am!"

On the other hand, we tend to think of the right brain as the more "feminine" side, the softer side. Art awareness is housed in the right hemisphere, as is the ability to interpret 3-D images. A particular kind of holistic insight can be traced to the right brain. Women tend to have more of this trait because there is more communication between the left and right hemispheres in their brains than in men's. And men have to work harder at 3-D imaging. The right side of the brain is the side of imagination, the part that is more analogical.

If we go outside, lie down on the grass, stare up at the clouds, and find a pirate ship shape in the white puffs, that's analogical thinking at work. Even though our left brain is telling us that the pirate ship is no more than a collection of water vapor made visible by sunlight striking it at a particular angle, our right brain is saying, "Ha, I don't care! Still looks like a pirate ship to me!"

Musical awareness is housed primarily in the right hemisphere. Most of the world's great piano tuners, oddly enough, happen to be left-handed men, which means they are right-brain dominant. There is something about a right-brain dominant, left-handed male that seems to accentuate the ability to distinguish tonal variations.

Why is all this important to a writer? Because as you delve into the writing process, you will sense the conflict or the contrast between the two hemispheres. You'll want to reduce things to their logical components when what your reader needs is not only the logic of the situation but the heart. One of my favorite quotes from C. S. Lewis says, "The two hemispheres of my mind were in the sharpest contrast. On the one side, a many-islanded sea of poetry and myth; on the other, a glib and shallow 'rationalism'."[3]

One of the reasons we want to use the visual in our writing is because it appeals to the emotional side of our brain. We should also keep in mind that the nerves leading from the eye to the brain are twenty times larger than those leading from the ear to the brain. In the course of your life you receive roughly twenty times the visual stimulation as you do auditory stimulation simply because the pipe is that much bigger. Because of that, we want to employ that sense of sight in our writing since it will excite memories that we have received and stored along the way.

Figures of Speech

Employing figures of speech can help make your writing more fun. Here are three types that you can play with as you're writing:

1. Pun—A pun is a play on words that sound alike but have different meanings. Matthew Chambers, a master punster, wrote this:

> Chief Inspector Blanchard knew that this murder would be easy to follow despite the fact that the clever killer had apparently dismembered his victim, run the corpse through a chipper-shredder, with some Columbian beans to throw off the police dogs, and had run the mix through the industrial-size coffeemaker in the diner owned by Joseph Tilby, the apparent murder victim. If only he could figure out who would want a hot cup of Joe.

2. Simile—A simile is an indirect comparison between unlike things using the words *like* or *as*. An example of a good simile comes from the Paul Simon song, "My Little Town": "*Saving my money, dreaming of glory, twitching like a finger on the trigger of a gun.*"

3. Metaphor—A metaphor is a direct comparison between unlike things where a figurative term is substituted for a literal term. In other words, it's a comparison that doesn't use *like* or

as. Musical and poetic lyrics use metaphors all the time, from Tom Cochran's "Life Is a Highway" to Song of Songs 2:1— *"I am a rose of Sharon, a lily of the valleys."*

Power Writing

When talking about great writing, even atheist literary critics have to mention the Bible. As the Word of God (who is the ultimate Creator of art), it's the finest artistry ever put on paper. It has every element of effective writing: powerful imagery, dialogue, visual language, similes, metaphors . . . the list goes on.

But one of the greatest aspects of biblical writing is its impact. The Holy Spirit, speaking to individual writers, understood how the human brain works and how we're more prone to remember simple things than complex. And when it comes to language, short, simple words often have more impact and power than multisyllabic, hippopotomonstrosesquipedalian ones.

> *Blessed is the man that walketh not in the counsel of the ungodly, nor standeth in the way of sinners, nor sitteth in the seat of the scornful. But his delight is in the law of the LORD; and in his law doth he meditate day and night. And he shall be like a tree planted by the rivers of water, that bringeth forth his fruit in his season; his leaf also shall not wither; and whatsoever he doeth shall prosper. The ungodly are not so: but are like the chaff which the wind driveth away. Therefore the ungodly shall not stand in the judgment, nor sinners in the congregation of the righteous. For the LORD knoweth the way of the righteous: but the way of the ungodly shall perish.*

Take Psalm 1, for example. In the King James Version, 73 percent of the text in this chapter is made up of one-syllable words. Why is this important? Perhaps one of the reasons this psalm is so memorable is because the words are simple. Now take a look at all the one-syllable words in Psalm 1.

> Blessed **is the man that** walketh **not in the** counsel **of the** ungodly, **nor** standeth **in the way of** sinners, **nor** sitteth **in the seat of the** scornful. **But his** delight **is in the law of the LORD; and in his law** doth he meditate **day and night. And he shall be like a tree** planted **by the** rivers of water, **that** bringeth **forth his fruit in his** season; **his** leaf also **shall not** wither; **and** whatsoever he doeth **shall** prosper. **The** ungodly **are not so: but are like the chaff which the wind** driveth away. Therefore **the** ungodly **shall not stand in the** judgment, **nor** sinners **in the** congregation **of the** righteous. **For the LORD** knoweth **the way of the** righteous: **but the way of the** ungodly **shall** perish.

Obviously, you don't have to choose your words simply based on how many syllables are contained in them. But isn't it amazing how effective Psalm 1 is using short, simple words? They're plain and yet they're graphic. They're clear yet creative. And at the same time, they create a rhythm, a meter, which makes the chapter even more outstanding as you read it.

> **The Lord is my** shepherd; **I shall not want. He makes me to lie down in green** pastures; **He leads me** beside **the still waters. He** restores **my soul; He leads me in the paths of** righteousness **For His name's sake. Yea,**

though I walk through the valley of the shadow of death, I will fear no evil; For You are with me; Your rod and Your staff, they comfort me. You prepare a table before me in the presence of my enemies; You anoint my head with oil; My cup runs over. Surely goodness and mercy shall follow me All the days of my life; And I will dwell in the house of the Lord Forever.

Seventy-six percent of the words in the Lord's Prayer have only one syllable. It's the most quoted prayer in the entire world. But part of its memorability is because of its simplicity, which is evident by the number of one-syllable words.

Love suffers long and is kind; love does not envy; love does not parade itself, is not puffed up; does not behave rudely, does not seek its own, is not provoked, thinks no evil; does not rejoice in iniquity, but rejoices in the truth; bears all things, believes all things, hopes all things, endures all things. Love never fails. But whether there are prophecies, they will fail; whether there are tongues, they will cease; whether there is knowledge, it will vanish away. For we know in part and we prophesy in part. But when that which is perfect has come, then that which is in part will be done away. When I was a child, I spoke as a child, I understood as a child, I thought as a child; but when I became a man, I put away childish things. For now we see in a mirror, dimly, but then face to face. Now I know in part, but then I shall know just as I also am known. And now abide faith, hope, love, these three; but the greatest of these is love.

Another memorable Bible passage is 1 Corinthians 13, the great love chapter so often quoted on Valentine's Day or at weddings. An astounding 80 percent of the words in this chapter have only one syllable. What does that tell us as writers? The most memorable writing is usually that which has the fewest words and the shortest words.

Tips from a Sample Letter

Though I certainly can't top the Bible's power and effectiveness in writing, let me offer an example of how you can put all these concepts together. It's a letter I wrote to my son, Gabe:

If you could hold this letter in your hand, you would notice that I've used a special kind of paper. It isn't that thick—at least a twenty-pound paper—it has a slight texture to it, and it's off-white in color rather than the blaring white you usually find. The goal is to make your letters special. The more personal and intimate, the better. That means you probably don't want to use anything that's ultra-slick or bright white like you would use for business correspondence.

As far as fonts are concerned, I like to work in a serif font most of the time. However, I composed this letter in a sans serif font to give you a look at what a sans serif font looks like. It's just a plain, ordinary, easy-to-read font that will communicate clearly, but with a bit more panache than a serif font. For sizing, I typically use a thirteen-point. I don't like to go any lower than twelve because it's not that readable.

Some of you will enjoy composing your letters on the computer. Others may want to handwrite them. Both are fine. But if you choose to write on the computer, there are some advantages. For one thing, you can design a letterhead like I've done. I started out with a graphic that I wanted my kids to see that said, "Yeah, that's Dad!" So I chose a lion, of course. Dad, the lion!

I also came up with a tiny logo under the lion. I wanted my kids to know the reason why I'm writing these letters. It's for the Word—that is, for the Lord Jesus, the living Word of God—that I write to them. I want the Lord Jesus to be glorified, so I capped my logo with a symbol that I wanted my kids to associate with Dad.

I started out with a personal greeting, of course, then the name of the child to whom I'm writing. I like to start out with a dramatic paragraph as an opener, so I started this letter out with a bang! You'll notice how I used short sentences and paragraphs. That creates a lot of white space, which makes the letter more visibly inviting.

My letter to Gabe has five short paragraphs, not including the address and the conclusion. I used dialogue in paragraph number four, and I also included my name, address, and phone number, just as a reminder to the kids. I like for them to be reminded, "Oh yeah, maybe I haven't called Dad in a while, so I'll dial him up." I then signed my letter with a personal signature. If there's a nickname your kids like to use for you, you can opt to sign it that way.

The key, again, is making the letter as personal to the recipient as possible. After all, it's all about sharing your love for them.

1 Chapman, Steven Curtis. *I Will Be Here*: Sparrow Records, 2003.
2 Duncan, Bryan. *When It Comes to Love*: Sony, 1993.
3 Lewis, C. S. *Surprised by Joy*, Harcourt Brace, 1955, p.164.

PRESENT YOUR TREASURED LETTERS IN A MEMORY BOX!

As you've read throughout the pages of this book, you've seen the power of delivering your letter in a *Memory Box*. One thing we've discovered is that without a treasure chest, you will surely lose your treasures.

The concept is simple: As you write letters throughout your lifetime, you will want your loved ones to house your precious letters in a *Memory Box* that *will last a lifetime, making it easy for them to find their letters and read them over and over again.*

We've made it simple for you to order and personally engrave your box today on our website and have it delivered to your home. *The Memory Box is the perfect gift for anniversaries, birthdays, weddings, holidays … the possibilities for giving this treasure are endless.*

Quite simply, it's a beautiful mahogany box that will hold something more precious to your family than any present you've given… *your words, your life.*

To my precious
Carolyn Sue Vaughn

Order at:
WWW.LETTERSFROMDAD.COM
1-800-527-4014

BRING *Letters from Dad*© TO YOUR CHURCH!

You hold in your hand the book...
Now catch the full vision.

Letters from Dad is more than a book. It's an experience. It's a wonderful new ministry that can be a part of your local church. We invite you to find out how you can be a catalyst to launch *Letters from Dad* in your church or within your own home. What a novel way to reach people with the love of God in your community: helping men to leave a Godly legacy of faith, hope, and love.

Every man wants a deeper relationship with his wife, children, and grand-children, and *Letters from Dad* will help you do just that. When you start Letters from Dad, you will:

- Meet in a **Legacy Group** of 12-14 men
- View the powerful four-part *DVD series* with founder Greg Vaughn
- Meet *once a month* for 4 months working through the curriculum
- Build deep and lasting *relationships with other men*
- Leave **treasured letters of love** that will be read long after you are gone
- Reach new people in your *community* with the *love of Christ*

It will be one of the most life changing decisions you'll make.

Your legacy adventure starts today –
Request your FREE information packet at

WWW.LETTERSFROMDAD.COM
1-800-527-4014